DO NO HARM

5 STEPS TO ALIGN POLICE ACTIONS WITH COMMUNITY VALUES

Ramon Batista
Mark D Ziska

CONTENTS

PART I

 ABOUT THIS BOOK

WE DESIGNED THIS BOOK to be flexible and friendly. You can use it as a reference book, flipping back and forth between sections that catch your interest. You can read it from start to finish. Or you can read the sections that interest you in the order you decide based on your needs. It's up to you, but we suggest reading about the history of policing first as it addresses the issue of character and how law enforcement has arrived at where we are today.

We hope that however you choose to read the book, you'll gain an understanding of who we are, what motivates us, and why we've written the book at this moment. We have a passion and a commitment not only to improving the way organizations run and grow, but also to helping people learn how to lead. How you arrive at your leadership goals with or without this information is up to you. We *will* tell you that enabling any organization to survive—and thrive—requires planning from the inside out. Thriving also means that the organization's leaders owe it to their employees and, for that matter, *all* of their stakeholders, to do everything possible to take advantage of the processes available to create effective plans to achieve the best possible outcomes.

This book provides a roadmap to build a better organization. Change may not be easy, but it is achievable—and we're here to show you how. We've had the benefit of achieving significant results within a police organization, and we hope the roadmap we share in this book will start you on your own path to organizational success. We're confident that our process will help all organizations, not just those engaged in policing.

Our intent was to create a book that would be of benefit to you now as well as in the future. Our greatest hope is that you will keep this book at the ready on your desk or nearby bookshelf and use it to make the kind of difference in your organization you wish to achieve. So, in the spirit of creating organizations that transform from the inside out, here's to your success!

INTRODUCTION

As a profession, policing is constantly evolving and regressing as we, as a society, struggle to find the best way to keep our communities and citizens safe. We feel badly for our good police officers who suffer from the actions of the bad officers. And we feel badly for all lives that have needlessly been lost to police actions. What's happening across the United States right now is not new. Understanding police history means not only understanding the roots of systemic racism, but also seeing how far we've come from those roots.

Policing in the US has gone through a series of transformative events since the first police departments were established in the 1600s. Colonial America's policing was quite informal—nothing like what we know as policing today.

A SHORT HISTORY OF POLICING IN THE US

Policing or community security among the colonies was based on a for-profit, privately funded system that employed people part-time.[1] A "night watch" was typical in most towns. This consisted of groups of volunteers who signed up to serve on certain days and times, primarily to be on the lookout for those involved in prostitution or gambling. (Night watches were established in Boston in 1636, in New York in 1658, and in Philadelphia in 1700.) We can assume the *values* of those watchmen were fairly tarnished, as it was common knowledge that they slept and drank while on duty. Worse, many communities put people on watch duty as a punishment—much like we'd put people in jail today.

Policing or night watch duties weren't exactly highly sought-after jobs. Early policemen didn't want to wear badges because they had bad reputations to begin with, and they didn't want to be identified as people that other people didn't like.[2] Compulsory police service, kind of like a military draft, was also tried. Those who were rich enough paid someone else to do it for them — usually a criminal or a local thug, which defeated the whole purpose.

Material Goods or Slaves

By 1838 Boston merchants had come up with a police model for security to protect their shipments of material goods as they moved from harbor to harbor, a precursor to the concept of protecting property of those in power.

During that same period, in the South, the economics that drove the creation of police forces centered on the preservation of the slave system. The primary policing institutions in the South were slave patrols tasked with chasing down runaways and preventing slave revolts.

In *The Evolving Strategy of Police: A Minority View*, authors Hubert Williams and Patrick V. Murphy cite historical sources that describe these patrols: "In Georgia, all urban white men aged sixteen to sixty, with the exception of ministers of religion, were to conduct such (slave) patrols "on every night throughout the year." In the countryside, such patrols were to "visit every Plantation within their respective districts once in every Month" and whenever they thought it necessary, "to search and examine all Negro-Houses for offensive weapons and Ammunition." They were also authorized to enter any "disorderly tippling-House, or other Houses suspected of harbouring, trafficking or dealing with Negroes." They could inflict corporal punishment on any slave found to have left his owner's property without permission.[3]

Historically our legal system sustained slavery, segregation, and discrimination. That, and the fact that the police were duty bound to uphold that order, is, we believe, responsible for helping to set a pattern of systemic racism for police behavior and attitudes toward minority communities that has persisted for centuries.

While it's true that important changes to policing professionalism, training, and culture have been instituted around the country over time, members of minority groups are still benefiting less than other communities from those changes.

If you consider today's media accusations that police are targeting black people, then it feels like we haven't come very far from our roots. That's exactly what the first police did—hunt black men and women.

Fast forward to the political model of policing in the 1900s. These departments ran afoul with the intrusion of politicians, the mafia, and street gangs into outright police policy. Corruption, excessive and daily use of force, and other issues made police work as dangerous and unpopular as it had been in the centuries before.

In Tulsa, Oklahoma, the late 1910s and 1920s were both financially prosperous and difficult. The African American community of the Greenwood District was among the city's most successful. Greenwood was considered the "Black Wall Street." According to the Oklahoma Historical Society, resentment raged in nearby white communities. Tulsa became a troubled town. In 1921, a group of vigilantes attempted to lynch a young black man. The sheriff and his deputies protected him and foiled the lynching.

As a result, a mob, many of whom were deputized by city officials, stormed Greenwood. They overtook the community, ransacking and looting businesses and setting them on fire. By nightfall, the community was completely destroyed. Martial law was declared. The deputized white vigilantes returned to their homes. African American citizens slept in the streets. Deep scars remained for some time.[4]

Over time citizen complaints led to a more professional model of policing. By the mid-twentieth century, Hollywood had also begun to shape the public's perception of policing. Remember Los Angeles Police Department detective Joe Friday in *Dragnet?* The TV series ran from 1949 to 1959 and again from 1967 to 1970. The timing was perfect. *Dragnet* introduced the concept of *values and crime* to nearly 75 percent of television-owning Americans. With an average of 16.5 million television viewers, and another 6 million radio listeners, the show's message that "police officers were courteous, clear-headed, and efficient, responsible executors of justice," made for great entertainment and shaped the perception of viewers—most of whom had no reason to think the LAPD was anything other than what they saw on television.

A 1967 Gallup poll found that 77 percent of Americans had "a great deal of confidence in the police," even while the facts showed the actual LAPD, on whom the show was based, disproportionately targeted people of color and used excessive force.[5]

Dragnet's message about values, the law, and fair treatment, and of course, Joe Friday's frequent demand for "just the facts," made for great public relations. But the real LAPD officers had a long way to go to demonstrate the values portrayed on TV in their daily encounters with citizens.

It's interesting that, at the height of *Dragnet's* popularity, race riots broke out in the Watts neighborhood of LA from August 11 to 17, 1965. After decades of racial tension, anger, and mistrust of the LAPD, all it took was one simple traffic stop to light the powder keg of frustration.[6] LA police officer Lee Minikus tried to arrest Marquette Frye for driving drunk after Frye failed a field sobriety test. Frye, and his brother Ronald, protested the arrest and things escalated. As more citizens began to join in more officers were called — resulting in more use of force, and riots.[7]

Over the course of six days, between 31,000 and 35,000 adults participated in the riots. Around 70,000 people were "sympathetic, but not active." The unrest resulted in 34 deaths, 1,032 injuries, 3,438 arrests, and over $40 million in property damage.[8] According to the *LA Times*, the Watts riots were the most severe in the city's history until those of 1992.[9] So much for Hollywood's *Dragnet* version of police versus Los Angeles reality.

Still, policing around the country was getting better, more professional, and more community-centered—at least until the Oklahoma City bombing in 1995 and the Olympic Park bombing in Atlanta in 1996. Those events began to turn the police focus toward the threat of domestic terrorism.

Policing shifted fully toward the threat of terror after 9/11. Much of the federally sponsored training, grants, and equipment that police and sheriff's departments received after that was in one way or another tied to preventing terror and quelling antiwar protests during the

Afghanistan and Iraq wars. The "warrior mentality" in many departments began to grow.

Ramon remembers this period like it was yesterday. In 2014, after the deaths of Michael Brown in Ferguson, Eric Garner in New York, and Tamir Rice in Cleveland, policing got another wake-up call about the use of force.

The President's Task Force on 21st-Century Policing

Give President Obama credit: he not only listened to what people were saying about discrimination and excessive use of force in policing, he reacted quickly to what he heard and took action, assigning a task force of law enforcement experts, academic professionals, and community leaders to address the issues. In spring 2015, the task force produced its *Report on 21st-Century Policing*. The president gave the task force ninety days to "identify best policing practices and offer recommendations on how those practices can promote effective crime reduction while building public trust."[10]

To date, it is the best roadmap for sensible, measured police reform. When the report came out, it promised hope and change, but that summer came the deaths of Walter Scott, shot in the back as he ran away from an officer (who planted a taser near his dying body) in Charleston, South Carolina, soon followed by Freddie Gray in Baltimore and Sam DuBose in Cincinnati.

DuBose was killed during a traffic stop by a college police officer. The body-worn camera video of the shooting did not support the officer's story. The officer was arrested, charged, and tried twice, with hung juries. That series of deadly incidents was very public and garnered a ton of attention. At the time, the Obama administration was also working overtime with the Community-Oriented Policing (COPS) office to push out the reform efforts suggested in the 21st-Century Policing report.

According to the report, the task force was "created to strengthen community policing and trust among law enforcement officers and the communities they served and both the report and the reforms were hoped to make a significant change in policing."[11]

The report was deemed critical, especially in light of the events around the country that kept bringing police violence to the public's attention. The report was invaluable in that it spotlighted the need and importance of lasting collaborative relationships between local police and the public. Many experts say it was "too little, too late." But Ramon disagrees—the report's timing was good. A series of other hurdles and roadblocks inhibited the success of reform implementation. The lack of focus on police values and community concerns were among the things that weren't addressed directly enough.

In *Why People Obey the Law,* Tom R. Tyler notes that "decades of research and practice tell us that the public cares as much about *how* police interact with them as they care about the outcomes that legal actions produce. People are more likely to obey the law when they believe those who are enforcing it have the right—the legitimate authority—to tell them what to do."[12]

What are we seeing now? People getting shot or killed because they don't respect the police, and they don't believe the police have the right to "tell them what to do." So, they resist, and like Jacob Blake and Charleena Lyles, many are shot or choked, and some die unnecessarily.

So, while the report was excellent, some chiefs and jurisdictions didn't fully buy into its recommendations. And some produced glossy reports saying they had done what it recommended (but not really). Before we knew it, the 2016 election was underway and the effort to fully implement the recommendations once again took a back seat to politics.

Enter the new administration in 2017. We found ourselves in a place where the COPS office was now hanging on by a thread. They had no influence on the topic of building strong community relationships; instead, the talk and focus was all about "violent crime" at a time when violent crime was at an all-time low. After the 21st-Century Policing report was published, and briefly caught the attention of those who truly cared about policing, talk of police reform never resurfaced.

The Department of Justice put one of the last nails in the coffin of police reform when they backed out of any proactive work on Title 42 United States Code Section 1983, brought about by the 1994 Violent Crime Control and Law Enforcement Act. The law gave the DOJ authority to investigate and hold accountable police departments that had strayed too far from the principles of constitutional policing.

Remember the slave patrols in the South? According to the Shouse California Law Group website, "Section 1983 was originally designed to protect slaves who were freed in the Civil War. They may have lost the war, but being intent to win the battle, Southern states began to pass laws that harassed and intimidated African Americans. Law enforcement officers in the South used their positions to assault victims."[13]

The law was passed as a part of the Civil Rights Act of 1871. The University of Minnesota Law School website notes that "Section 1983 provides an individual the right to sue state government employees and others acting 'under color of state law' for civil rights violations. Section 1983 does not provide civil rights; it is a means to enforce civil rights that already exist."[14] This act of Congress allowed black victims to file a lawsuit and recover monetary damages. That lawsuit could be filed in federal court. This allowed the victim to avoid state court. In state court, the victim would likely have faced a strong bias.

Now the [really] bad news: because police departments didn't heed the warnings regarding establishing trust, the use of force, community policing, and culture and diversity in policing, we find ourselves where we are today—with news of George Floyd, Michael Brown, Eric Garner, and others, as well as citizen responses to those incidents. The list is growing, and it's not going away until we change our approach, our values, and our strategy and tactics.

If police leaders, jurisdictions, city managers, and mayors don't implement better policies and accountability, then predictably we'll find ourselves in an ongoing series of bad outcomes. African Americans and others will continue to die in situations where they shouldn't be dying.

New abuses will all be caught on smartphone video and the riots and protests will continue; police will continue to be targeted, ambushed, and abused; and policing and community safety will get even worse. Citizens will stop trusting police, departments will be defunded, as indeed some already have; and crime will spike.

Understandably, state legislatures are moving forward at warp speed. In some cases, we worry that they're not slowing down to examine the entire set of outcomes. As an assistant chief and police chief working to improve policing, Ramon is a student of policing history. The national riots that erupted in the 1960s, the pre- and post-reports from that era spelled out what needed to be done, and guess what? Those changes didn't happen. The policing profession is on the cusp of a new era of reform. Change is coming. We must embrace it and help shape it, lest we sit back, arms crossed, and have the changes imposed on us.

KEY STATISTICS AROUND POLICING TODAY
Up to 50 percent of Police Fatalities Involve the Mentally Ill

According to a recent report by the nonprofit Treatment Advocacy Center, "People with untreated mental illness are sixteen times more likely to be killed during a police encounter than other civilians approached or stopped by law enforcement."[15]

Many of these calls result from individuals with undiagnosed conditions or mental illness of the person that police and first responders are unaware of when they answer a service call. Mental health calls, known or unknown when officers are dispatched, are the situations most likely to go bad.

The Treatment Advocacy Center notes:

> While about 3 percent of US adults suffer from a severe mental illness, they make up a quarter to one-half of all fatal law enforcement encounters. . . A recent internal review by the Los Angeles Police Department reported that 37 percent of police shootings last year involved suspects with documented signs of mental illness.[16]

According to Statista.com, in 59 cases out of a total of 118 reported mass shootings, the shooter(s) displayed prior signs of mental health problems.[17] The vast majority (95.7 percent) of jails the center surveyed reported having some inmates with serious mental illnesses from September 1, 2010, to August 31, 2011. Of the 49 jails surveyed, 21.3 percent reported that 16 percent or more of their inmate population were seriously mentally ill. Larger jails reported having larger proportions of these inmates. The survey further showed that 31.3 percent of large, 13.2 percent of medium, and 4.2 percent of small jails reported that 16 percent or more of their inmates had a serious mental illness.[18] Sadly, jails have become the de facto treatment center for those suffering from mental illness. Every single one of these inmates encountered a police officer—some more than once—prior to incarceration.

What's the solution? It is complicated, but not impossible. More training for officers in how to identify and deal with mental health issues is but one basic step. More collaborative work with mental health professionals and the deployment of police/crisis intervention specialists is another. Building multidisciplinary teams to address those experiencing serious mental health issues is a better bet than sending two, three, or four police officers to every call involving a person in crisis expressing suicidal ideations. We're willing to bet that most officers and community members would welcome the idea of diverting initial 911 calls to mental health professionals for triage before dispatching police officers. Regardless, we must all be prepared to accept that the police will not be decoupled from mental health crisis calls until these new systems can respond effectively at 3:00 a.m., and even then, the fact that some encounters can instantly turn violent, jeopardizing the safety mental health clinicians, means that the police will likely continue to respond with them.

Police Calls Are Mostly Nonviolent

The Department of Justice crime stats as well as individual department statistics such as New Haven Connecticut's Computer-Aided Data report 95 percent of police calls are non-violent. Again, only about 4.6 percent of all police service calls involve assault, gunfire, robbery, rape, stabbing, murder, or person shot.[19]

The most common calls for service fall into the category of traffic accidents, motor vehicle stops, parking complaints, noise complaints, trespassing, criminal mischief, welfare and door checks, mental health complaints or requests for help, physical health checks, vandalism, drugs, prostitution, and domestic complaints, among others.

Prior to the protests and disturbances across the US following George Floyd's death, police work was not as exciting and non-stop drama like Hollywood would have us believe.

In 2018 the DOJ reported:

- Residents aged 16 or older who interacted with police in the preceding 12 months fell from 26 percent in 2011 to 21 percent in 2015, a drop of more than 9 million people (from 62.9 million to 53.5 million).

Police-initiated contact decreased by 8 million (down 23 percent)

- The volume of people who initiated contact with the police dropped by 6 million (down 19 percent)

- Contact from traffic accidents did not change significantly[20]

Police-Initiated Contact

Of the 223.3 million US drivers, 8.6 percent experienced a stop as the driver of a motor vehicle.

- A greater percentage of stopped drivers were male (10.2 percent) than female (7.0 percent).

- Blacks (9.8 percent) were more likely to be stopped than whites (8.6 percent); Hispanics (7.6 percent) were the least likely to be the driver in a traffic stop.

- In total, only 1.0 percent of persons experienced one or more street stops while in a public place or parked vehicle.

- A higher percentage of blacks (1.5 percent) experienced street stops.

- When police initiated the contact, blacks (5.2 percent) and Hispanics (5.1 percent) were more likely to experience the threat or use of physical force than whites (2.4 percent). Males of any race were more likely to experience the use of physical force (4.4 percent) than females (1.8 percent).[21]

These numbers show a pattern and tell a story. Communities are paying attention, now, police departments and their leaders must heed the signals for better policing. Remarkably, at the same time, citizens are actively asking for the police to help them thwart violent crime, but they want the police to do it in a fair and just manner. Simply speaking, communities don't want to be hurt by the same people they look for help.

THE CHALLENGE OF CRIME IN THE US

Currently there are 328.2 million people in the US and even though only a fraction of the population wakes up every morning with intent to harm their fellow human beings, these individuals present a significant threat to communities all across the country.

Some say serial killers are rare: only thirty to fifty are in circulation at any time. Researcher Thomas Hargrove, however, estimates there are almost 2,000 serial killers at large in the US, undetected and hunting their next victims. Whether it's 50 or 2,000 killers, do we really want to defund the police? The men and women working to find, apprehend, and arrest these people and the thousands of other criminals who kill, rape, and assault citizens every year would simply vanish, leaving citizens to fend for themselves.

Then there are those whose crimes consist of non-violent acts such as illegally selling cigarettes, passing a bad $20 bill, blocking the street, doing drugs, running from police, or simply living their lives and engaging in low-level property crimes.

In a country born out of revolution, it would not be surprising that some people are in possession of weapons. They may be under the influence of one or more legal or illegal substances. They can be drunk, combative, or have a criminal record or outstanding warrant. They have broken the law, but they can hardly be called evil as the justice system and most officers define the term.

Every year a few of these men and women make the news, not because of their crimes, but because of how they die: at the hands of police officers and the use of force while controlling or attempting to control a suspect. The general public is keener than they are given credit for: they can discern differences in the use of force to subdue an evil man's deeds versus those of the person stopped for "jaywalking."

In the latter, the use of force, and often a resulting injury or death, leads to public backlash and loss of trust in the police. Resentment and discord between the police and the public is greatest in areas that have seen the cycle of perceived unfairness and excessiveness endlessly repeat itself. The difficulty in all this is the human element. The great majority of officers are well-intended, good people doing a terribly difficult job. An officer is on the spot making life-and-death decisions in seconds, cases that most often take months and years of deliberation. You could have a great culture that emphasizes the sanctity of life (they live it), yet still have tragedies due to the circumstances. There could be a police officer in any culture who willfully *breaks the rules* knowing full well that they shouldn't have. Those are easy cases to spot and prosecute because the officer obviously displayed carelessness in their conduct.

As Mike Tyson said, "Everyone has a plan until they get punched in the face." Police officers are fallible human beings, not superhuman robots. In this critical juncture, a well-intentioned officer makes a bad decision and someone loses their life.

An Opportunity to Improve

The public is demanding that police leaders acknowledge all the shortcomings and move with urgency to fix it. Defunding the police is not the solution, the answer is in the development of a sound strategic plan, hiring for values, character, and heart of service. We believe that good funding leads to diverse recruiting, hiring and most importantly better training.

Based on our experience, our time and the results we had in a major city police department, we know our strategic planning system works. We also know that one of the most important strategies to create a successful department is hiring for lived values and a heart for service, followed by other strategies that include: training your departments, holding officers accountable, and then creating and implementing a detailed strategic plan with accountability for all initiatives, projects, and training/performance skills. We've done it. We've seen the results and now we want to help other departments achieve the success we've had.

THE POLICING CHALLENGE

WE'VE TALKED ABOUT THE history of policing and the importance of values, but there are many problems facing law enforcement today—too many to list in one book, let alone one chapter. So we've chosen to address what we believe are the top five problems in most agencies and our five-step solution, including a strategic plan, that addresses them.

PROBLEM #1: ACHIEVING TRUST AND LEGITIMACY IN THE COMMUNITY

The final report of President Barack Obama's Task Force on 21st-Century Policing lists six pillars as the underpinnings of 56 recommendations for improving and reforming policing in the US:[22]

- Building trust and legitimacy
- Policy and oversight
- Technology and social media

- Community policing and crime reduction
- Training and education
- Officer wellness and safety

Aptly, the first pillar is building trust and legitimacy: these are the foundational elements for police in a democratic society. The challenge to secure these elements is ongoing. Police departments will never be able to claim completion in this arena because the work of building strong resilient communities is never-ending.

Like raising a child is a lifelong endeavor, albeit one that should become easier with age and proper parenting, it's never over. There will always be opportunities for growth, change, support, and failure in every department. And, there will always be another generation to raise once the previous generation matures. The officers we train today will be training their replacements in a matter of years.

Trust and legitimacy are the foundations of success for a police department, both externally and internally. They're also the toughest obstacles and are the greatest challenges that so many departments experience. The same way that over decades of history, communities have lost trust in police departments, so too have rank and file members lost trust in the organizations they work for.

Rebuilding internal trust will require a re-examination of the common bonds and culture among members of an organization. We must ask: why do you exist, what brings you to stand together? Core beliefs and values are the foundation of mutually agreed values and mission. Without them, and an awareness and acceptance of them, no trust or legitimacy can be formed.

Therefore, before a police department sets off to build trust in the community, it has to build trust within the ranks. Organizational trust takes time and a deliberate effort to be transparent and collaborative with its members while strengthening and building a culture that believes in the greater mission of public safety.

PROBLEM #2: MOLDING POLICE AND COMMUNITY CULTURE TO ACHIEVE TRUST AND ALIGNMENT

Problem #1 correctly identifies the President's Task Force on 21st-Century Policing mandate of establishing trust and legitimacy as the first pillar. However, Ramon disagrees with the task force's recommendation that officer wellness and safety should come last. Sequencing, focus of importance, and positioning matter: Pillar #2 should be officer wellness and safety.

It is imperative for the long-term health of a policing organization to invest and ensure that their officers are mentally and physically fit to deal with the rigors and stress of policing in the US, the land of the free, and a country with over 300 million guns. Americans acknowledge that the police have difficult jobs, it is our belief that we can only expect them to perform at a high level, if we have invested in their wellness.

You can't have unparalleled service to your community until your officers have a vision of providing unparalleled service to others. What does full-service policing look like? The work of trying to achieve alignment within the organization in order to get you to where you need to be is immense. You can't get anything going if you don't get the members of the organization to see the vision of where you want to be. Those two are very inextricably linked.

PROBLEM #3: WARRIOR VERSUS GUARDIAN MENTALITY

The Army Warrior Ethos states, "I will always place the mission first, I will never accept defeat, I will never quit, and I will never leave a fallen comrade." That ethos is the mindset called a "warrior mentality." That ethos is a set of principles by which every soldier lives.[23]

Police values are military values. According to the Department of Defense,[24] the core values of each branch of service are

- **Department of Defense:** Duty, integrity, ethics, honor, courage and loyalty

- **Air Force:** Integrity first, service before self, excellence in all we do

- **Army:** Loyalty, duty, respect, selfless service, honor, integrity, personal courage

- **Coast Guard:** Honor, respect, devotion to duty

- **Marine Corps:** Honor, courage and commitment

- **Navy:** Honor, courage and commitment[25]

The military and police both operate on a belief that core values not only govern how individuals act within the organization, but how they guide the actions of those individuals as they do their jobs. While we share values, the critical aspect is how those values are lived, practiced and enforced, and the mindset behind the values.

In policing, the warrior mentality is necessary in a small fraction of an officer's career, while the majority is taken up by practices that require good interaction skills such as empathy, listening and the capacity to think through a problem and find pro-social solutions. That said we cannot discount the need for men and women in uniform that are ready and able to display courage and bravery when it is absolutely necessary to protect themselves or our communities.

Among the recommendations of the 21st-Century Policing task force was the promotion of a *guardian mindset* over the *warrior mindset*. Almost seven years later, the debate about the two continues. The task force's report urged, "Law enforcement should embrace a guardian rather than a warrior mindset to build trust and legitimacy both within agencies and with the public."[26]

Many, including police officers, question the semantics of the term, but as Val Van Brocklin pointed out in a

Police1 article, "Words matter." She wrote that Lieutenant Chad Goeden, commander of the Alaska DPS Training Academy, began implementing a guardian mindset when he first took command of the academy there. He specifically instructed his staff to stop using the term *warrior* and begin using the term *guardian*.[27] Why?

The definition of guardian is a "defender, protector, or keeper"—one who advocates for another. This approach to providing public safety and living by the values we've listed above, which ultimately means a change in mindset, can help build trust between officers and civilians and prevent the unnecessary use of force.[28]

We're interested in the warrior/guardian debate because of how *all* mindsets go back to values and living one's values. Aligned values lead to great police work, individual values in opposition lead to the problems we've seen. Values determine not just the success of policing, but of business, life, career, and all the decisions human beings make.

With time, good or bad values will affect and change any culture. We're seeing that happening in the US right now. What normally happens is there's not enough attention paid to those values on the accountability side. We can put our espoused values up on the wall or make fancy documents, even speak about the department's values, but if we're not actively living and checking ourselves on those values every day, then we are missing opportunities to grow and get better as individuals and as an organization.

The values set and communicated by top members of a business or organization are sometimes disconnected and not personally or professionally meaningful: "Yeah, that's what we say, but that's not really what we do." Have you heard that? We have. Once you set solid foundational values, then you have to begin to apply them in your officers and live them yourself if you want to see them take root and grow. Eventually, that new culture, that new way of doing things and living by those values will take hold. But it's a long journey.

Your values are the things that you believe are important in the way you live and work. They should determine your priorities, and deep down, they're probably the measures you use to tell if your life or department is turning out the way you want it to. You need a strong chief, a strong leader who can articulate the value, communicate it, and apply the consequences for not abiding. You can make it work, but people are often reluctant to be open-minded about it, especially if they sense a loss of power, have deep-held beliefs (in their mind, they are right and the new proposals are just wrong) or have different ideas about how that value is upheld.

The culture we are part of when we develop our values also becomes the culture and method we use to *drive* our values. We can all have the same values, it's how we choose to uphold or implement those values that matters—especially when the event is highly charged, or emotionally volatile. For example, applying the value

"Integrity," it's doing what's right at all times, even when no one is watching, whether emotionally charged or routine situation.

PROBLEM #4: UNDERSTANDING POLICE UNIONS

Support is a rare and valuable thing in any profession. It should come from the top and encompass everyone in policing that has the opportunity to influence or lead change, it includes the police chief, the union leadership as well the elected officials. Law enforcement leaders and police union *leadership* should work in concert as willing and active participants in the chief's strategy. At their core, we believe that chiefs and union leaders understand how and where officers get (or many times, lose) public support, therefore it is critical that they join forces to support positive change efforts. The work of a chief and police unions in recognizing this time in history, as the time to act together can't be overstated. Their priority of the moment should be on rebuilding trust and forming citizen bonds that continuously build support for our officers. The broader the tent, the greater cross section of the community you reach, the better.

We acknowledge the difficult balance for police unions. On one hand they must support their union membership in times of crisis, that is their charge, as public servants, they are also charged with upholding their oath of office. The union's role has come under intense scrutiny after police actions in places such as Rochester, New York; Kenosha, Wisconsin, and Minneapolis.

Indeed, the majority of Americans question the union's ability to see what we've seen. In reality they may be seeing exactly what we have seen. The public may be at odds with the union's public positions. Then there was an aha moment, like it or not, the union is performing its legal obligation.

Early in his career as a company labor relations representative—his dream job growing up—Mark was befriended by a crusty and difficult union business agent. Let's call him Al. He said, "Mark, you can't just take management's side and say the employee violated the rules and should be fired. It's your job to understand, and to stay above the fight. Be reasonable and ask why. *Why* did it happen? Listen, just show you care. Then don't fall for my bluster and positioning, don't get pulled in. Just listen. You're not the one facing federal charges of failure to represent, but I am."

"A charge can deplete the union's budget. Yes. It's the law. A union must represent each and every employee. We're like a defense attorney. We take our client as they come, right or wrong, guilty or innocent. The union will always come out strong in support of the employee. But if you listen you will hear how we really feel about the case. You'll understand which cases we push because a person *is* innocent and which cases we're only fulfilling our duty under the law for. Got it? Listen. Listen, and

together we will do what's best for all parties involved."
Al demonstrated his value of family—the union family.

Often those people who have the most difficulty at work or the most problems at work become the most vocal opponents of departmental leadership. They are the ones who work to undermine confidence in the values the organization's leader and members hold. Again, it gets back to values, lived values, true leadership and character. Are they living the values? If not, what are the consequences?

This lack of support becomes a strategy to gain power or diminish another's power—no matter who that person is. It's all about achieving power. When there are no consequences, guess who holds the power? They do. Don't abdicate your responsibility to create and enforce aligned values!

Some of the old guard currently in power undermine the existing, or any proposed strategy in order to retain power, or to prevent a shift in power. Even politicians, along with city government, will undermine the strategy, no matter how effective or good for a department the changes might be. Why? For a variety of reasons:

Local government might not have the stomach or the skills to deal with the issue so it's easier to just ignore it. Other forces move in to take advantage of this reluctance to face the issue. This is true among more departments nationwide than we like to think about. As a matter of fact, when people begin to lay the blame on unions, everyone should take into account that it was city leadership, elected officials and police chiefs that entered into those union agreements. In turn, unions do what they are charged with doing, representing their interest, their membership.

We've seen that same power struggle with police reform in Congress, deadlocked between the proposals in the House and Senate. However, several states have taken up their own versions of police reform, notably Colorado, New York and California. Legislators in thirty-one states brought forward approximately 450 police reform bills. Our concern is that if police leaders do not recognize the reform era of policing and quickly work to address the shortcomings and emphasize the goodwill of the profession, they will be in a position where their officer's work is being crafted through hastily drawn laws.

Like so many issues, reforming police work will require thoughtful reengineering in the social network, addressing issues such as homelessness, drug addiction and mental illness, to name a few. This is a moment of crisis and opportunity for our profession and police leaders need to step up and show courage to acknowledge that we can and will do better to address our community's concerns.

PROBLEM #5: DEVELOPING A STRATEGIC PLAN TO CHANGE A DEPARTMENT

Many police departments are well intentioned: they have a vision, but haven't clearly defined a path to get where they want to go. Our five-step process can help your department create a strategic plan. Even with the other problems—lack of support, police culture, lack of values alignment, and a warrior mentality that sees the community it protects as the enemy—a strategic plan can, over time, change a department.

If you have a challenge not listed that you'd like to see addressed, contact us so we can incorporate it in our program. For more information, visit www.donoharm-book.org.

MEET THE AUTHORS

HAVING A HEART FOR service and a proven passion for people doesn't always come across on a resume. A resume or bio only tells one part of a person's story. Understanding where we came from, what drove us and what still drives us will tell you more about this book and why we wrote it than anything else we could say.

Our official credentials are also listed at the end of the book for those interested. This book is about more than strategies, tactics, and plans. It's about people—the people and agencies who put it all on the line to protect US communities every day—and how to help them continue to do that, only better.

RAMON BATISTA:
MY JOURNEY TO BECOMING A POLICE OFFICER

If you'd told me when I was a kid growing up in the south side of Tucson that one day I'd be the patrol captain for that same neighborhood, and then chief of police for the city of Mesa, Arizona, *I would have believed you.*

I would have believed you because I was one of those kids who deeply *wanted* to be a police officer. I *wanted* to help people. The fact that I didn't have any avenues, opportunities, understanding about policing or the faintest clue as to what I needed to do to get where I wanted to go, didn't stop me. No matter what challenges came my way I kept dreaming. The day I graduated from the police academy, a friend asked me how I felt, I told him it was incredible and that I would be the chief of police. My friend laughed and told me to focus on the upcoming field training program, I laughed as well, but deep inside I knew I had the determination and grit to one day achieve it.

Growing up, I would try to get a better understanding of what police work was like by riding my bicycle up to officers who were doing traffic stops in my neighborhood. Even as a little kid, I'd try to engage them in conversation. I don't know what kind of success I had, to be honest with you, but I kept doing it.

One time, unexpectedly, while riding my bicycle, I got pulled over by an officer right in front of my house. He wasn't very friendly. He asked me where I lived. There I was, a ten-year-old in complete awe of the police, but at the same time being semi-interrogated about where I lived. I responded innocently, "Right here," because I was right in front of my house. That encounter didn't deter me from wanting to be a police officer.

Later, as a teenager, I got pulled over while driving. The officer who stopped told me that it was because I matched the description of somebody that they were looking for. Many years later, I figured out that that was something that police officers sometimes say to justify their pulling you over. I had not committed a traffic violation and still, I got pulled over.

It was a combination of those experiences that began to form my understanding of what it's like to be profiled. But at the same time, it didn't deter me. I held steady in my desire to become a police officer and if anything, it gave the awareness of what it is like for a kid to be pulled over by the police for no good reason, and how those experiences (repeated over time) can shape a person's view of the police. I look back on my meager beginnings and my experiences with the police as a genuine gift. Those memories guided my career and influenced my philosophy about how police officers should interact with everyone, not just those that support the police at every turn.

I had to wait until I was in the middle of my teens in order to join an "Explorer Post," where I began to learn about policing. That helped. That experience cemented my belief that policing was something I wanted to do. From there I was committed.

When I finally did become an officer, a lot of those things made sense to me. Nonetheless, it was really disappointing when I came to the realization that even though

I had joined a fraternity/a family, there was still a divide that was not readily visible until you experienced it.

As a member of a minority group, it is hard to explain unfair situations, when you sense that although all things are equal, you are treated a little differently and you always have to work harder to achieve your goals.

Unfortunately for me, the way I experienced it at times was when I would compete for opportunities, but be passed up for them. I knew full well that all the qualifications were the same; the only thing that was different was how I looked.

That awareness came full circle once when I was in a locker room of a police substation. Two officers were having a conversation. They weren't aware I was there, or that I could hear them.

One said to the other, "Hey, I wanted you to know that I'm really looking forward to the opportunity to put in my memo of interest to be a field training officer." The other guy, who was the one that oversaw the program, said to him, "Don't worry about it. You're in. You're in." You could hear in the other guy's voice, his realization, that "oh, I'm good, I'm in." *Memo schmemo* I thought to myself.

Here I was. I genuinely, always wanted to be a field training officer, I wanted to do my part to affect the future of our workforce. I looked at my career path as holding multiple hurdles that you had to go through if you were a minority. You had to make sure you had all of these qualifications and check marks in your resume. Yet here these two guys were having this conversation where the legitimacy of the process was painfully laid to bare.

It was disappointing to hear that kind of talk—to come face to face with it. Still It didn't deter me within the organization. I always sought and, to this day, still seek equity for everyone. I knew that unfairness existed.

Although I don't think it was pervasive, I think it was still a barrier that had to be overcome for myself as well as for others like me. I wanted to make sure I did everything that I could to level the playing field for everybody.

It didn't matter to me what anyone looked like. I just wanted to make sure that everyone had a chance that was transparent, fair and not based on relationships, race, or some other bias. To this day, I believe that practicing internal fairness is a cornerstone to developing a trusting organizational culture.

That was my early-to-mid-career life as an officer. I spent the first ten years of my career as a line-level officer—a patrol officer. But upon that tenth year I thought, I've been a patrol officer for 10 years. My friends who went through the police academy with me are becoming detectives or sergeants. They're moving up the ranks and I'm still doing officer work.

At the time, I thought I had better get going, but I was having so much fun in all aspects of being a police officer. I had special assignments, I had a lot of training, and I did become a field training officer. The time really flew by me. In fact, it didn't really come full circle to me as to how much I appreciated that time until I became an assistant chief and a police chief.

Then I had the proven experience and knowledge of understanding what it's like to be a patrol officer. I was somebody who had risen through the ranks from patrol all the way to becoming a chief. That's important because one of the biggest complaints against police chiefs from patrol officers is, "Hey, you don't know what it's like."

In this case, I knew exactly what it was like and could relate to our officers' experiences of being everyday patrol officers, dealing with societal dysfunctions that stemmed from years of systemic government neglect in disadvantaged communities, moreover today's police officers are functioning in a criminal justice system they did not build.

Most police officers are well-intentioned people with a calling to help others. Officers working in a patrol function today came into the profession in the post 9-11 world of anti-terrorism. The events of domestic terror that included the Oklahoma City bombing in 1995 and the bombing of concert goers at Centennial Park during the 1996 Olympics in Atlanta, were the precursors to the shift in training, funding and focus for local, state and federal law enforcement; lest we forget that it was the federal government that provided the funding and the training.

That work was vitally important to protecting the homeland, but it also hastened the shift away from what really works in keeping our cities safe—community-oriented policing, full-service policing, and problem-oriented policing.

I became a detective, then a sergeant, and stayed in those ranks for quite a few years. I was a sergeant—a first line-level supervisor—for seven years before I took the next promotional opportunity to become a lieutenant, which is a mid-level manager. I stayed at that rank for about five years.

I then got into senior management as a commander and a captain overseeing an entire patrol division, with about one hundred officers in Operations Division South, in the neighborhood I grew up in. At the time, it was forty-seven square miles with about 120,000 residents, of which approximately 98,000 were Hispanic, my ability to speak, read, and write Spanish was very helpful. It was amazing to be the patrol captain in what was my neighborhood. Here I relived story after story from my childhood around every corner. I also had an amazing opportunity to lead police officers and the community helping build stronger bonds.

I worked hard in Operations Division South to build the morale of the officers assigned to that area while building relationships with the community. This is when I realized I had a real strength in connecting with people in everyday situations. They trusted me. That came with a heavy burden of making sure that if I said I was going to do something, I knew I had to follow through.

My focus was on engaging with people, following through on my word, and continuous, as a result, building trust. I knew the onus was always on me to make sure that I delivered what I said I would.

I started to realize that, at times, it was quite a burden to not only perform my daily obligations, but also step up to develop leadership skills that would further support the community. I found, if I was not careful, I could overload myself with promises that I might not be able to deliver on.

It was in that timeframe that I realized I had the possibility of becoming a chief. I worked with dedication and persistence eventually getting assigned into difficult areas. The chief recognized that I had a leadership skill set, and therefore assigned me as his chief of staff in his office. I was still a captain. It was from that position as his chief of staff and overseeing the daily operations of the chief's office that I was promoted to assistant chief. By then, I had my education in line. I had my undergraduate and graduate degree and I was seeking every opportunity I could find for executive level type training.

I attended the FBI national academy in Quantico, VA for three months, and I studied at the University of Boston for three weeks in the Police Executive Research Foundation's Senior Management Institute for Police. In essence, I pursued every opportunity to prepare myself for the rigors and the challenges of being a police chief, including the Major Cities Chiefs Association and Police

Executive Leadership Institute where I was paired with a seasoned big city police chief.

With three decades of experience, executive-level training, and mentors along the way, I knew I was ready to be a big-city police chief. I had a lot of ambition, but I was looking for that next level edge. I knew that as an assistant chief, trying to become a police chief, managing a team in the thousands of people and budgets in the tens of million dollars was going to require more insight. I needed to learn from people who were experts, who understood strategy and preparation and how to think in terms of the big picture.

By the grace of God, I had the opportunity to meet Mark through a school superintendent in Tucson. With his coaching and help, I went on to successfully compete for the police chief position in Mesa, Arizona. Mark knew my background and understanding organizational behavior, Mark was somebody that I kept going back to, saying, "Hey, I'm seeing this. What do you think?"

I was trying to figure out what the department believed in. I was trying to understand what was important to the organization. I was trying to focus them around a core belief, the core values that I believed the department stood for.

That's how those conversations with Mark and I started, and that's how the greater work went on to transform that department. Out of that collaboration came the five steps, strategic planning, and success we experienced firsthand through our work at a major city police department.

As I said early on in this book, throughout the 1990s and my time as a patrol officer, I saw communities burn down. I'm seeing it happening again. As history shows us public revolt is almost always tied to some type of police action that the public views as either excessive or an unfair application of the law.

I lived through the aftermath of Rodney King. I know firsthand how the actions of officers thousands of miles away can have a negative impact on a well-intentioned officer trying to do the right thing in another city. If someone smarter than me dusts off those old crime commission reports and reads them aloud today they will think they are in a time-warp. They'll see the same complaints about excessive use of force, with the same calls for police reform. The only things different are the names of the victims, the cities, and the dates.

It's been one heck of a tough career. I guarantee you that I had nothing given to me. Everything required work, persistence, and the experience of making mistakes, picking myself back up, learning from them, and then, over time and practice, getting better. That's okay because I appreciate it that much more.

MARK ZISKA:
MY JOURNEY TO BECOMING A POLICE ADVI

I grew up in a white, affluent suburb of
have an African American person in a
until I got to college. However, when I
years old, there was a group of three or four African
American young men coming down our street. I had not
seen an African American in our neighborhood before.
I remember being a little afraid and using the "N" word.
When I used the "N" word, like lightning, my father gave
me a backhand and said, "Never will you use that word
and never will you disrespect another person." There was
more to it than that, but that's what I remember about it.

I thought a lot about it, why I said what I did and where
that racist thought had come from? It didn't come from
my home. It had to have come from my community. It was
all around me. It was in the people that I hung out with.
As a seven-year-old, how many people are you exposed
to? You're exposed to your friends. I probably got it from
them and they got it from their parents. To me, that is a
systemic form of racism.

From then on, I never used the "N" word again, but I
still had that little bit of worry. If I see a group of African
Americans walk through our University of Arizona neighborhood, where they may also live, I still have a little bit
of that cringe, that fear that occurs. It's likely in many of
us white males of my age, it developed in our early youth,
like a lot of our social culture.

ame to think if it's in me, it's very likely in others. e been on enough ride-alongs to know that it's in many police officers too. We've talked about values, culture and race. I'm not alone. There are many others like me who experience this or hold even more egregious views. I don't choose to reinforce these views, but they exist. It's in our culture, it's learned.

It's in our society, and our social system, and it's going to take a long time to get it out. I believe being aware of these views and taking personal action to change our own behavior is the best place to start. This is change that comes from within, from our awareness, and our desire to change.

Then the question becomes: do police officers some-times have that same feeling and respond in a way that is more focused on feeling than thinking? I think it depends on the way they were raised, their values, and their char-acter as people.

I was raised in a family where my grandmother did a lot of my raising. My parents both worked. My mother was the secretary to Mayor Hubbard of Dearborn, Michigan. It was a very racist community. We didn't live there, but in a suburb outside of Detroit. Dearborn was an all-white com-munity that made it clear that no blacks were allowed. This was in the 1950s and 1960s, before civil rights laws tried to put an end to some of the structural racism that took place. People there made it very clear that they did not want an integrated neighborhood. Dearborn was a working-class city and also a wealthy city because of Ford Motor Company. The city was able to buy out a big lake outside of the city. They built cabins and a recreational area for people who lived in Dearborn. However, no blacks were allowed in Camp Dearborn. Like I said, Dearborn was overtly racist.

Not everyone who worked for Ford or lived in Dearborn was a racist, however. I chose to get into Human Resources because of my grandfather. He was a union organizer at Ford Motor Company. He ended up getting a gold watch from Ford that's engraved by Henry Ford II thanking him for his thirty-five years of service. He told me many stories of management abuses. In one, during the Depression, he had to bring his foreman's laundry home and have my grandmother wash it and dry it overnight. This was in the winter, so she couldn't hang the clothes outside. She had to go in the basement and put extra coal in the furnace, open the grate and let the heat come out into the basement so she could dry the clothes. Then she would iron and fold them so he could take them to work the next day. He said he had to do that a number of times in order to keep his job.

After listening to those stories, I knew I wanted to get into labor relations. I got introduced to organizational development and saw the value of psychology in the workplace. My graduate degree is in industrial psychology. I started to get the bigger picture of how when you get everyone aligned and working together, you can accomplish far more than if you have people who are divergent and divided. It's just like a country. If people are divided, you can't achieve as much as if people are united.

I specialized in organizational development, got a coaching certificate and I had a chance to understand how HR operates as a system. When I work with executives, I help them think of their organization as a system and you have to make sure every part of that system is healthy. From that, I came up with the competencies and the competency star I describe in more detail later in this book and on our website. That competency star demonstrates in a visual how the organization is a system when it comes to the people in a system and competencies and having the right ones to achieve your outcomes.

DO POLICE VALUES MATTER?

Have you watched the news lately? It's mostly reports and videos of disturbances and protesters. What's on the media's mind right now is crime, violence, police shootings, and the calls for justice around the country. But this unrest is not new. This has been going on for more than three centuries. It will continue to happen unless things change. Fewer officers, less training, and reduction of resources won't change the things that need changing. The talk of defunding the police only pushes the police further away from meaningful engagement.

If you look at the last fifty years of policing, as we have—and understand why we decided to write this book—you'll notice the one thing that does make a difference in policing, in business, and in our personal lives: our *values*. What do we hold dear, and what determines our success in life? Having and living good values—integrity, honesty, courage, trust and service to others—is the way to effect change.

Nothing will make a difference in law enforcement until we change the kind of officers we recruit—hiring as much or more for values, character, and a heart for service than we hire for policing skills. It is much easier and more effective to hire an officer who aligns with a department's vision, mission, goals and philosophy than it is to train someone to fit.[29]

Pair value hiring with implementing a strategic plan with goals to achieve the kind of communities we want to work and live in: safe, equal, supportive, and non-violent, and then things will change dramatically. Safe communities mean safe officers and vice-versa, two arcs moving in the same direction, not away from each other. In fact, the further away that police and communities drift, the more dangerous it becomes for both groups.

We've seen our strategic process work, and we think getting it out to other cities and departments will enable their agencies, communities, and cities to implement the same kinds of change. Change must begin in our core values as officers, as politicians, as people, and as a nation. We're willing to start with ourselves and our officers and trust the rest will follow. It begins with one critical action—learning.

Always be learning. What you need to know tomorrow comes from what you learn today. That's true for business, it's true for school, for life, and especially for policing where what you learn today can save a life tomorrow. This is the reason why you sometimes hear us say/write that this would be a great reference book for aspiring police chiefs.

THE LIGHT AT THE END OF THE TUNNEL

This topic, this book, and the fate of police departments across the US are critically important to us and we believe, to our country. We've painted a dark past and a gloomy view of the origins of policing—not because we think policing is doomed. It's not. It's because we believe that only by looking back can we see how far we've come and how much we've improved; and we have improved, even though it doesn't often look that way.

The use of force is a contemporary issue in policing. It's not an issue that's going to go away. We're talking about how to start the process of building an overall solution, and a foundation that can start anew to address this issue and others. What we are proposing in our book is the bridge to get us to the other side of a difficult divide.

Like we've said, we can see what's happening from both sides of the equation. If we can get you to step back for a second and realize that the profession of policing is entering a new era, much like the history of policing has seen before, this new phase can aptly be called the "reform era."

Instead of recoiling when we hear the words "reform," we should acknowledge, embrace, and help shape the future of policing. We see the abundance of good, the bad, the media, and the citizenry weigh in on all topics police and security related. We have concluded that we should be focused on strategic plans that include transformation, education and training in each community.

Based on our experience, we know our system works. We also know that one of the most important strategies to create a successful department is hiring for values, mission, vision, and goals alignment[30] [31] followed by other strategies that include: training your departments in de-escalation practices such as Integrating Communication and Tactics (ICAT) by the Police Executive Research Forum, building transparent policies that outline the expected norms of conduct, holding officers accountable, and then creating and implementing a detailed strategic plan with accountability for all initiatives, projects, and training/performance skills.

We've done it. We've seen the results and now we want to help other departments achieve the success we've had. But first, an important question to ask yourself is: what are the top struggles you, and other departments are facing right now? This is what we've found:

More than 99.9 percent of police officers wake up and get ready for work with the intent to serve humanity. They get up every morning with intent on doing good, saving lives, and helping their community. They have no intent to hurt citizens in their communities—even those posing a risk to others.

Somewhere in the moments of leaving home and arriving at work, those 99.9 percent of officers think about the risks associated with their profession. They are focused on helping citizens, not hurting them. However, some days, in spite of all their training, experience, and consciousness, everything that can go wrong does go wrong, and someone dies.

As a police officer, as Ramon got ready for work every day, those thoughts crossed his mind. He knew that wearing a gun and a badge meant that that day could be the day his faith, his courage, his skills, and his experience were tested. He could die. He could kill. He could kill and be killed. Things could go horribly, horribly wrong, and spiral out-of-control in seconds. And he couldn't do a thing about it, except rely on his will, faith, and training to pull him through.

That's the reality of life for all officers everywhere. Just as citizens get in their cars, go to work, or school, and about their lives every day, not anticipating disaster or accidents—life, for better or worse, happens to us all, except this specific risk factor of facing a situation where you may have to use your weapon in a life/death case is exponentially higher for police officers. You hope and pray that if and when the bell is rung, you will be at your best as you answer the call.

It's not just the officers who worry. Their families share the same silent burden of "what if?" All of them cling to their faith in their spouse, father, brother, sister, son, or daughter who is an officer. They trust that they will be careful and that their training, decisions, and actions will guide them safely until retirement.

Every year, through a twist of fate, time or circumstance, thousands of officers are placed in situations where they must choose whether or not to use lethal force. Whether they choose yes or no, these men and women will have their lives and the lives of the community members changed forever. Not only must they live with the organizational consequences and the community consequences, but also a personal "hell" that they can never fully recover from if they take another human being's life.

Officers take critical actions from a string of decisions they must make in a matter of seconds, or minutes—always under pressure and usually while highly stressed, decisions that require the courts, months and years to review and decide on the best practice. Those decisions can have dire consequences. A shooting could end their career as well as life or lives. Even in the most lawful shooting or situation where the officer is right to take their actions, they will still live with questions. Like the victim's family, they too will ask, "what if?"

The community wants officers to protect them from evil and the day-to-day issues of domestic violence, mental health problems, drugs, addiction, traffic accidents, and the whole realm of police service calls. Life is not perfect or safe.

We also want officers who excel at non-violent encounters such as dealing with the homeless, helping the person who has overdosed or who needs medical attention, showing empathy, providing a listening ear, a helping hand, and access to resources—not a citation. These are the competencies we seek at all levels. These qualities are the basis for hiring, recognition, and promotion.

We want good people with high emotional quotients (EQ) and skills, as well as good physical, decision-making, and leadership skills. The law enforcement profession has to lean-in and be a part of the solution, building multi-disciplinary teams to tackle community problems that have a component tied to laws and the criminal justice system. A forward leaning police department will recognize that they cannot arrest their way out of problems borne out of deep societal ills.

These are the competencies at all levels. They are the basis for not only hiring but for recognition and promotion. And finally, we want men and women with that crucial "heart for service"—a core belief in helping people coupled with a drive, passion, and commitment to serve their community. Ramon also wants to see a "guardian mindset," where officers are trained to be safe without approaching every citizen as a potential enemy combatant.[32] The majority of the public wants the same thing we do. They want to feel safe and secure from crime as well as the officer's actions.

Collectively, we need to see past the smoke and noise generated between supporters of the thin blue line and the Black Lives Matter movement. In all reality, officer safety translates into community safety and vice/versa. These should not be opposing beliefs or a binary choice, the resiliency and strength of a community starts with the bond between the police and the communities they serve.

They want to feel and be protected by their police departments. Contrary to what the media portrays about defunding the police, the majority of Americans—81 percent according to a recent Gallup poll, do not want the police defunded and would like to see more police in their neighborhoods.[33]

The mission of policing in a free and democratic society is to provide public safety services in a manner that reduces or eliminates harm to the community, and to those who break the laws of that community. Another goal is to mitigate or reduce incidents of and complaints about excessive use of force.

That's the reason we titled this book, *Do No Harm*. Ramon's vision as chief of any police agency in the country, large or small, is to first, "do no harm" and strive for "no harm" with the knowledge that policing, even when done perfectly or close to it, is still a high-risk prone endeavor. That said, our policies and leadership are focused on public safety and the best outcomes where both the community and the police walk away from highly charged events safely.

OUR VISION FOR POLICING IN THE US

Given the events around the country, the civil unrest, the protests and the calls for action, we see this five-step process as the fastest (not overnight, but within six months to a year), most doable option departments have to make a significant difference in their community and their agency.

At the end of the day, what we're trying to do is reduce as much of the risk and harm to our citizens and communities as possible. At the same time, we're trying to create a guidebook for aspiring police chiefs or leaders in the private sector that want to figure out a strategic roadmap for improvement within their own agencies. If you ask us what our vision for police departments in the future look like, we would say that we want officers, whether newly out of the academy, or with decades of experience, to look at how they can create or help create a police department that "does no harm."

If you are in one of these categories, or if you're a city manager, community member, or are just interested in a police model that reduces harm to citizens, immigrants, criminals or suspected criminals, keep reading. This book is about how you go from wherever you're at now to a higher, more peaceful, more focused, and community-centric state, one that can remain safe for the public and the police. Hopefully, this book will provide you with some wisdom in how to accomplish that.

PART II
THE FIVE STEP
PROCESS

STEP 1:
IDENTIFY YOUR VALUES

I've done a lot of executive coaching. After years of practice, what I've seen is that the people who are willing to open up and look inside themselves, to honestly examine their values, and to be intro-spective are the people who get the most out of coaching and the most success out of life.

—*Mark Ziska*

1.1 A VALUES-DRIVEN LIFE: A VISION FOR COMMUNITIES, BUSINESS, POLICING

Officer Gary Lynch shared this story with us:

This guy was a very, very big man and we were told he was carrying a weapon. We'd gone to arrest him. I knew he had been very, very vio-lent in the past. He had been in prison and now he was going back to prison. We went into the house and stepped slowly down into the dark back basement where he was sleeping. He had a blanket over him so we didn't know whether he had a weapon under there or not. I went up beside him and I quietly said, "If you have a weapon, things are going to go very, very badly for you."

Of course, I never would have hurt him. I just wanted him to think that's what I would do if he had a weapon (to gain his compliance). I then told him very matter-of-factly that he just needed to comply with me. He got up. I placed handcuffs on him, two sets because he was such a large man, and we walked out to the car without incident. I seated him in the back seat and rolled the windows down. I tried to make him as comfortable as possible. I knew he was going to prison. He knew he was going to prison. We went out to the Pima County Jail.

I'm a tall man, but he must have stood almost a foot taller than I was. As we started to walk across the lot he looked down at me and said, "Do you know why I didn't fight you? Because you treated me like a human being."

I said, 'Wait a minute. I told you things would go very badly if you didn't do exactly as you were told to do."

He said, very matter-of-factly, "Oh, that? That's just you doing your job."

That was his attitude. He had fought with many, many officers in the past—and I'm certainly glad he didn't fight with me because I would have been no fight competition for him whatsoever.

I tell that story because it demonstrates what I know to be true: that no matter who you are, or how long you've been on the job—just treat people the way you want to be treated. That makes such a difference.

We share Gary's story because it demonstrates what *we* know to be true: that at its core, good policing begins, depends on, and embraces our values. Values determine culture, define policies, and predict the kinds of issues or successes a department will have with its officers. Values are the basic and fundamental beliefs that guide or motivate our attitudes, actions, decisions, and choices.

Our values determine our personal success or failure in everything we do—from our career choice, how well we move on our career track, to our marriage, relationships, and success in society. Values help us to determine what is important to us. Whether good or bad, values are the motive and reason behind every purposeful action, decision, or choice we make or take.

Gary's values come from his faith in God. He also told me that he believes God placed him in the position he was in. His faith-based values include treating people the way you want to be treated: no matter how bad they are, or how they're acting, or what they're doing. Personal faith, religion, or a spiritual belief are just *one* of the places we *get* our values.

Our family, culture, upbringing, and personal experience can also form a foundation for our values. You don't have to have faith in God to have values. But you do have to have and live your values to be a good officer.

Officer Sean Payne is also a man of faith. He teaches classes at the local police academy on how to treat others:

> It's really simple for me. I just believe that everybody, no matter how bad of a person they are or what they've done, deserves to be treated with respect and dignity. My thing is that when you're dealing with someone who is aggressive or angry, that might not be the real person you're dealing with. It could be mental illness. It could be associated with narcotics or something like that. They could be a really good person normally, but they're just going through a hard time at that moment. What I've learned is that if you do treat these people with respect when you encounter them again, even if they're at their low point again, a lot of times they'll remember you.

A month ago, there was a guy who was fighting with officers in a house. The tone goes off and we're all en route to go help. He happened to be someone that I dealt with about four months ago. I treated him right at that time, and I was honest with him. Give them water if they're hot. Just do whatever you can do to treat them like you would want to be treated.

As soon as I walked into the house, he saw my face and stopped fighting. He said, "I'll deal with Officer Payne," and he turned around, putting his hands behind his back. "Officer Payne can handcuff me."

It's not that I'm a super cop. It's just because of how I treat people.

How We Treat Others Matters

How we treat people. Think about that for a minute. How often have you reacted defensively or angrily to being treated poorly? How do you react or feel when you are treated well, especially if you're not at your best?

You know it makes a difference to be respected and treated with respect and courtesy versus being ignored or treated disrespectfully. And that's if you're in a neutral or good frame-of-mind at the time.

If you feel the difference between respect and disrespect as you're going about your everyday life, imagine you're drunk, angry, out-of-control, or having just caused an accident or been caught committing a crime, and then being treated with dignity and respect. What does that do to your mood? How does it impact your actions, or your anger or fear?

Showing respect and dignity to people, no matter what's happening to or with them in a moment are powerful values. I'm not saying people will immediately change as these two prisoners did. I'm saying you're making an impact now that will most likely make life better for someone else—including you or another officer at a later date dealing with the same individual, small actions like this, lead to safer communities tomorrow.

Values Matter

It's not just policing where values matter. Values determine an individual's or organization success as well. Even further values:

- Help mold a culture, where standards are high and fear is low.

- Go beyond the urgent, ethical leaders take action with a view toward the long term, upholding the values of the culture.

- Guide leaders' choices so that their every action which is watched by many, helps reinforce or improve the desired state of their organizations.

There is no question that the ultimate goal of any organization is to build a values-based culture. To this end, success will look like a stable, collaborative working environment that, over time, will be characterized by productivity and employee commitment to the values and thus the organization.

Take Adam Fridman, the founder of ProHabits, who first noticed there was a connection between successful people and a company's values. He found that people and businesses who lived their values were ultimately more successful. He decided to dig deeper and see if there was a correlation between values and success.

He was surprised to find there really was a link. His team evaluated 2,057 values gathered from a total of 397 organizations and found five top values seen across Fortune 500 companies. His research showed that the top values of Fortune 500 Companies like Apple, Amazon, and Microsoft had a definite link between their *lived values* and their organizational success.[34] The top five values were:

- Integrity
- Teamwork
- Innovation
- Customer service
- Respect

These aren't just shallow buzzwords. They're actual values that create real-life success wherever they're deployed. For example, when Eric Christopher, CEO and producer of BizFamous Media Group asked Tony Hsieh, CEO of Zappos, what he would do differently if he were to start his company over again, Hsieh said, "If I could go back and do Zappos all over again I would actually come up with our values from day one. We actually didn't always have values. It wasn't until about five years into it that we rolled out our values."[35]

Hsieh ended up selling Zappos to Amazon for $850 million in 2012.[36] At that time he stated that if he could do one thing differently, it would be to create the company's values at the very beginning. What does that tell you about the importance of values? If values are that important to a company that sells shoes on the Internet, how much more important is it for a police department who deals in potentially life altering situations with people, good and bad, day in and day out?

While values like trust, loyalty, respect, customer service, and integrity are touted almost everywhere, it's certainly not the case that they're always successfully lived out. In fact, even if people could tell you what their values are, not many could tell you they consciously live them every day, which brings us to the important steps of how to identify, determine, prioritize, and then *live* your values.

Identify Your Values

Police values are often found in police tradition. For example, truth, integrity and respect for others are often values police associate with especially when making difficult decisions.

When you *consciously* identify and choose strong, positive values, you are also choosing a life that is more purposeful, both personally and organizationally. Not identifying your values is like not identifying your skill sets. Personal values offer a critical source of direction for everything you do.

EXERCISE 1

Use Figure 1 to identify your top values. First check off all values that resonate with you. If there's a value you don't see, add it to the list. Don't overthink this. After you have finished, group all similar values together from the list of values you just created in a way that makes sense to you. Don't worry. You're the only one who will see this unless you choose to share it.

Next, create a maximum of five groupings of words. If you have more than five groups, re-evaluate them. Finally, choose one word within each grouping that best represents the label for the entire group. Again, don't overthink this. It's not a quiz. There are no right or wrong answers.

Example:

Grouping of similar values. For example: Abundance, Wealth, Financial security, Freedom, Independence, Money. The one word in this group might be **Freedom** because financial security and money gives you the freedom to make choices to gain the things you want.

You can change the words based on what resonates most. The five keywords from each group are most likely your five core values.

The goal of this exercise is to examine your values and commit to five key, core values. Don't race through this. It might take hours or days. Pick it up, work on it, set it down, think about it, take your time get to know yourself. The point is to begin to be aware of what is important to you, and what values you use to make decisions. Maybe you joined the police force because you wanted to help people. Maybe you joined for the adventure and excitement and to be more than just another employee somewhere. Maybe you like the idea of a job that's different every day. Of course your choice of values could be a combination of these as well as additional reasons. Below is a list of values to consider.

VALUES LIST

Achievement	Advancement	Adventure	Affiliation
Authority	Autonomy	Balance	Collaboration
Community	Competence	Competition	Connection
Contribution	Cooperation	Courage	Creativity
Economic prosperity	Economic security	Empowerment	Fame
Family	Focus	Freedom	Friendship
Fun	Giver	Happiness	Health
Helpfulness	Honoring	Inner Harmony	Integrity
Involvement	Knowing	Knowledge	Loyalty
Making a Difference	Non-Judgement	Order	Personal Development
Pleasure	Power	Quality	Recognition
Responsibility	Safety	Self Motivation	Self respect
Service	Spirituality	Success	Trust
Wisdom			

Figure 1. Align your individual values with organizational values

The next step is to align your employees' personal values with the overarching collective values of your organization. Once you create an alignment of shared values, you create the organizational resilience to tackle the tough issues and thus set all stakeholders involved up for success with creating long-lasting culture change.

Tough Questions
Following is a checklist of questions you can use to assess where you are around building an effective values foundation:

- What are your department's values?
- What are *your* top five values?

- Is your organization and departmental culture performance-enhancing?
- Are you supporting, encouraging, and rewarding officers who live their values?
- We discussed them earlier, but we're revisiting them here because they're the foundation for everything from the plan to the tactics.
- Could you write your values down right now, or would you need to think about them?
- Could your officers and/or co-workers list their values without thinking about them?
- Do you know where they came from?
- Do your family and friends share your values, or are you the guy/gal who is constantly teased for being "good"?

Determine Your Value Priorities

Tom Landry, former head coach of the Dallas Cowboys, told the team what his priorities were and that he expected them to share them, and the values they came from. His values were "Faith, Family, Football, Fans."

As one of the greatest coaches the game has known, you'd think football came first. But it was third. Over the years his players have shared many stories where faith and family trumped football in his life and theirs.

We share that story because we think it's important not just to know your values, but to know what their *priority* is in your life. By prioritizing your values you'll determine how you'll spend your work time, and your free time and what decisions you'll make on and off the job. Your prioritized values create the measurement you can use to tell if your life is turning out the way you want it to. The top five values you pick will be the most important. These are the ones that impact your daily decisions.

For example, If your top value priority is focusing on your family, you will make different choices when it comes to promotions, jobs or opportunities, that would take you away from time with your family. If your job security, money, and commitment to the community come before family—maybe you're young and single for instance, you'll make different choices. By knowing *what* you value, and *why* you value it, you'll be able to make the right choices and decisions. Your values can change, so re-evaluate them every six months or annually or when you're feeling conflicted. The important thing is to be aware of your values regularly to make sure you are integrating your values into your daily life.

Live Your Values

There's a quote from the movie *The Matrix* that we both identify with when it comes to values. Morpheus tells Neo, "Neo, sooner or later you're going to realize, just as I did, that there's a difference between *knowing* the path and *walking* the path."

Knowing something is different from *doing* something. Nowhere is this truer than with our values. Knowing what values *are desirable* is different than *acting on and living* our values. Living our values gives our lives both true direction and meaning. There are different kinds of knowledge. There are things we know with our heads—facts, words, data, phrases, etc. This is called "knowing the path." Anyone can learn facts, procedures, and processes. This knowledge is what we store in our brains. Then there's heart knowledge, or "walking the path."

Walking the path means not just knowing our values, but consciously and deliberately *living* our values. Walking the path means not just knowing *what* to do, but understanding on an emotional level *why* we do it. For instance, an officer may "know" that all human beings should be treated with respect and compassion and have no problem doing that, but an officer who "lives" that knowledge understands *emotionally and personally* as well as mentally what it means to treat people with respect and compassion—regardless of the forces acting on them to do otherwise.

If, for instance, you're not a parent, you may understand that mothers and fathers tend to be extremely protective of their children. That's head knowledge. Once you have your own children however, you truly understand where that protective sense comes from—it's in your heart as well as your head. You *feel* it and understand it from an entirely different perspective.

Knowing you should treat the prisoner who just vomited on you and took a swing at you, with dignity and respect is one thing. Doing it while your jaw is throbbing from the impact, and while wiping their spit from your face is another. If your values aren't embedded in you, it's going to be difficult to summon them in times of stress.

Most of us will say we have values, but do we live what we say? You don't get apples from lemon trees. It's not our words, but our actions that matter. It's our actions that prove we're not all talk. If you want to know what an officer's values really are, you look at their actions, their personnel file, their reputation among their peers—not their words. People live their values and our true values play out in our actions, our character, and our lives.

Living your values means having a relationship with your values. You can't just sit down and list your values and say, "Okay, that's done." A relationship with your values means you think about them. You reflect on them when you're challenged to do or say something that makes you uncomfortable.

Here, you ask yourself:

- What is important to me in this situation?
- What larger purpose do I stand for?
- Will my values be strengthened, weakened, or ignored if I do this?
- Is the choice, decision, or action I'm about to take in alignment with my value of _____?

These questions will become automatic when you truly understand and live your values.

Living your values needs to be a natural outgrowth of your daily life with coworkers, team members, family and friends. One of the stories Ramon particularly likes is from officer and police academy instructor Sean Payne. Sean was making good money in real estate, but then decided to take a pay cut to become a police officer. His values were his faith, providing for his family, community, and service.

Choosing to become an officer was easy for Sean when he looked at his values that aligned with his desire to serve. And though the opportunity would come with a pay cut, his wife who also placed family as a top value, supported his career transition. It wasn't easy but they both made personal and financial sacrifices to help. Sean further lives his values of faith, family, and community guided him into the career he's been very happy with since.

Sean Payne and Gary Lynch are models of what we want in modern day police officers. Men who are driven to do the right thing by their values, in the best of times and in their most challenging times. In a moment of crisis, we would want a professional officer, one that upon opening the door, conveyed professionalism, caring, understanding and courage to tackle our concern; in that moment in time, police officers like Sean and Gary epitomize an ideal police officer. Police officers that function like Sean and Gary are out there every day; the organizational challenge before us is to harness them into an overwhelming force for good.

Six Practices of Proactive Leadership

In an article for the *Harvard Business Review*, Robert Chestnut described six practices for leaders who want to be proactive—or live their values:[37]

Lead by Example

Leaders need to maintain integrity at all times. Employees will see when your integrity isn't upheld. One act of non-integrity, no matter how small, will outlive the stories of one hundred acts of integrity in the minds of your employees. You have to walk the talk or risk undermining the time, effort, and resources you've invested in your strategic plan and any departmental changes.

Once your employees see you're not, or not always a leader with integrity, any future change efforts will be near impossible to accomplish and sustain. One slip, one "Well, just this once," attitude will bring down years of credibility.[38]

Make Your Ethics Code Your Own

Personalize your values and ethics, as well as those of the department. There is no such thing as a good generic code of ethics. Your values and ethics need to be personal and unique to your organization. As Chestnut said, "Values need to be personal. You can't outsource integrity."[39]

Talk About Your Values, Ethics, and Integrity

Talking about your values doesn't mean bragging about them. It means a simple, humble conversation about values and action. In other words—tell stories! In order to both normalize and ingrain values, integrity, and ethics into your departmental culture, you need to normalize them. There's no better way to do that than by encouraging the practice of telling stories. Storytelling, sometimes called "narrative," gets people's attention. We write police reports the way we do because they're for a legal audience. But when we want our friends or colleagues to understand what happened, we tell it like a story. If you were the audience to this story, Which one would you rather read/hear:

Police Report

"On 5 July 2020, 5:00 p.m. I observed a red Ford Fiesta driving into and over stop signs along a five-mile section of Fordham Road...At each stop sign the car knocked down, the driver would stop, the horn would sound, and the driver would scream 'Stop' out of the window. I initiated lights and siren and directed the driver to pull over and stop on the right shoulder of the road."

You can imagine how the report proceeds from there. Just the facts. Now, imagine your colleague says:

Personal Narrative

"It was crazy. This woman was knocking over stop signs, blowing her horn, and screaming 'I said 'Stop!' each time she ran over a sign. By the time I get her to pull over I can tell she's obviously drunk. I can smell the alcohol before I get to the car, and she is feeling no pain. She's crying and so I ask her what's going on. That's when I saw the gun on the floor. I had her get out of the car... I came to find out she just shot her boyfriend in the leg for sexually assaulting her and not listening to her when she said 'stop.' ..."

Both narratives tell a story, but the interesting story people will remember will be the one told from a personal perspective, about what the officer felt, thought, and what values they used in dealing with the situation, not the report version. By openly discussing values, as well as the struggles and questions employees have through storytelling, you create a culture that reinforces that values, ethics and integrity are normal and important.

You can discuss values by sharing experiences, relating stories about events that happen to you, and helping colleagues make sense of their experiences and environment through storytelling—much like we do when having dinner or hanging out with friends.

A recent *Forbes* article explains that stories are "the natural instrument of change, because they draw on real events by real people in a real way. Stories come from the experience of the people who act, think, talk, discuss, chat, joke, complain, dream, agonize and exult together, and who collectively make up the organization. By contrast, conventional management focuses on lifeless elements – mission statements, formal strategies, programs, procedures, processes, systems, budgets, assets – the dead artifacts of the organization."[40]

Through storytelling about your community and group work, police leaders and their officers can co-create their values. Their stories help create a cultural shift in the organization's culture. When it comes to policing, the right story, told well can mean the difference between "an offender focus [and] victim-centric" perspective. Likewise, the view of law enforcement's work with the community can begin the shift in earnest, where the police view themselves as the collaborative caretakers of their communities. The short definition would be "guardian."

It has been found that efforts to "subtly insert an organization's values" into conversations has been seen trickling down the hierarchical chain. Leaders need to believe in the organization's values. Otherwise they won't be able to get others within the organization to do the same. Additionally it creates distrust and stops rapport from developing.

Macaulay & Rowe (2020) found that after a department implemented the use of storytelling, community members saw officers were more empathetic and victim-focused, and less focused on investigations. "Officers within the department were able to break away from a fear-based environment that punished mistakes, and was punitive in general. The environment became less of a "command-and-control hierarchy," and learning from errors became part of the norm. An effort was made to encourage and support officers, decision-making became more effective, innovation and "managed risk-taking" increased."[41]

Sharing stories can be a beneficial tool for talking about values and ethics as well as culture, work, and family. Stories help create shared values within the department. The more hierarchical levels engaged in narrative or storytelling the stronger the value system will be. Narratives also help with values being integrated into officers' words and actions on a more consistent and daily basis.

The New Zealand Attitudes and Values Study (NZAVS) is a twenty-year longitudinal national probability study of social attitudes, personality and health outcomes of more than 60,000 New Zealanders. The NZAVS is led by Professor Chris Sibley, and is unique to New Zealand.[42]

Mark is particularly fascinated by this study because it explores how New Zealand Police used storytelling in order to affect a major culture change in police departments.[43] The study used evidence from over 240 semi-structured interviews. The research challenged each participant's current thinking about police cultures. The study showed how allowing members of a police agency to develop and share stories promoted attachment to new cultural values, through sense-making—the process of giving meaning or insight to something.

The results of the study extend the current literature on co-creation and co-production, and the impact of storytelling on power relationships in organizational culture. It suggests that the crafting and sharing of stories enables value-attribution in a co-creative environment.[44]

Make Sure People Know How to Report Violations

We know that ratting out other officers is intensely frowned upon in police culture. But integrity demands for people to have the courage to do the right thing. Edward Burke reminds us that "The only thing necessary for the triumph of evil is for good men to do nothing." It's important that the culture supports and encourages (appropriate) reporting.

Employees must feel safe holding colleagues and leaders accountable or they won't report them. As Chestnut said, and we concur, "No individual within an organization should be exempt from being held accountable for behaviors that counter ethics and integrity."

To date, the New Orleans Police Department's Ethical Policing Is Courageous (EPIC) program is one of the best, aimed at putting the responsibility of keeping fellow officers out of trouble in the hands of the officers themselves. Through EPIC, the officers are trained in a peer intervention program that was created with the help of New Orleans community members. The main focus of the EPIC is to educate officers on how to intervene and prevent an unjustified action from occurring. In my view, EPIC is a modern-day tool for surviving highly charged events; events that if gone unchecked can lead to the loss of a career or worse, a criminal complaint.

It's also important that agency values are clearly communicated to the public, either online, via social media or department websites. Doing so conveys accountability. If the community is aware of your values, they can question events that are incongruent or seem counterproductive to them through a reporting process they can easily access and utilize.

Demonstrate the Consequences

Employees and stakeholders aren't trusting what you *tell* them. They're watching and trusting what your *actions* show them. Transparency, internally and externally around investigations and enforcement of the consequences will build trust inside and outside the department. The ultimate purpose of police departments is to provide safety and security. Police accomplish their main goal in concert with the people they serve. The police cannot accomplish the most basic task if they do not have the trust and belief of their legitimacy in the eyes of the community.

In the short term it may upset people and create dissent, but in the long run it will show that accountability does result in changes, and that no one is exempt from the rules. It will ultimately send a strong message about values and strengthen your agency. When people know they can trust their leaders to do what they say, they feel safer, become more loyal, and perform better. The precept of accountability should be second nature in policing, one of the main functions for police officers is to uphold laws and others accountable.

Remember That Repetition Matters

You can't just launch a program, talk about your or your departments values, and then walk away. A launch is not self-sustaining. You must consistently reinforce the fact that integrity, values, and ethics do matter. This is why these things need to be embedded in the culture, demonstrated through stories, and discussed regularly and in relevant ways.

Not only does repetition and utilizing creative and varied means of delivery keep your message and the values from getting stale or annoying, it drives home the point that integrity isn't a fad, and that values matter.

Critical Core Values

Turn on the news or get on social media and it's easy to see what values the media and communities *think* the police embody. Video of tragic outcomes between the police and the communities they're supposed to protect, serve as a canvas that begs for change. Those events and the systems that caused them should be addressed and rectified, but they do not embody the totality of well-intended police officers in this country.

In fact, the reality, according to polls and studies, is that the majority of police officers value serving, protecting, and creating safe communities and show it every day. The majority of citizens support the police, value their efforts, and prefer increasing funding for training rather than defunding or eliminating officers and departments.[45] So, where have we failed, how badly have we failed? What needs to change?

We believe what needs to change are departmental values, officer values, and a strategic plan for closing the performance gap with hiring for values.

1.2

We like to think of values in terms most of us can understand, as our personal DNA. DNA is what makes us uniquely us. The main role of DNA in the cell is the long-term storage of all kinds of information—from determining who we are physically, to remembering events and responses we have as we grow. A Nature Neuroscience study showed that mice trained to avoid a specific smell, similar to the smell of cherry, passed their aversion to that smell on to their offspring.

Experts conducting the study said the results were important for phobia and anxiety research. They showed a section of DNA responsible for sensitivity to the cherry blossom scent was made more active in the mice's sperm. Both the mice's offspring, and their offspring, were extremely sensitive to cherry blossom and would avoid the scent, despite never having experienced it in their lives."[46] That's not all. Changes in brain structure were also reported: "The experiences of a parent, even before conceiving, markedly influence both structure and function in the nervous system of subsequent generations."[47]

So, our DNA can tell us if we'll be short or tall, muscular or lean and wiry, healthy, or prone to disease. Our hair color, temperament—it's all encoded in our DNA. However, not so obvious characteristics, as one study shows, are also in our DNA. Our tendency to vote, or not vote, and whether we vote liberal or conservative, and even our values are in our genetic makeup. Biology is not destiny. While our DNA combination is a result of our parents, and of their environment even before we're born—as well as our environment after we're born, it's not permanent. We can change, but our DNA is still the starting point for everything we think, what we believe, do, or how we act.[48]

The same thing is true of our values. Values aren't *just* about what or how we believe, or how we think we should act. Values are how we *actually* act. If a person says they value honesty, but lies all the time, honesty is not a true value.

If someone says they value family, hard work, and loyalty, but their life doesn't reflect those things, their true values aren't family, hard work, or loyalty. You can't get apples from a lemon tree. You can't get caring and service from someone who doesn't embody those values. They can act, or pretend to have them, but when it's critical to act on them—they fail.

Our values, conscious or not, determine who we become, how we respond or react to life, and what choices we make. A lot of organizations and businesses talk about "having values," or values in general. But not many organizations or people really sit down and look at what their values are. We believe even fewer look at how they're implemented. Few organizations consciously make hiring decisions based on candidates who hold and live shared values. But this is where solid organizational success comes from It's not lip service. It's real.

1.3 A HEART OF SERVICE

Companies and agencies and businesses are built, consciously or not, on their underlying beliefs about what matters to them. If a company says they have "great customer service," but their customer service is marginal or spotty, they don't truly value great service or it would show in their actions.

If officers say they value de-escalation, and having a "heart of service," that's great. But if citizen complaints of excessive force are prevalent or on the rise, one begins to question their stated values around peace, community, respect and dignity. There may be another disconnect that is not readily apparent, regardless, it's time to sit down and reexamine the values with them to make sure they are all on the same page regarding what matters to them, the department and their community.

To understand where our values come from, begin with examining your own beliefs. The quality, type, and the number of our values will ultimately be determined by the source of our beliefs. Those beliefs may come from our family, our faith, our culture, or our environment, but in general, they tend to be imposed by our culture or environment and then strengthened or reinforced over time by the people we work and socialize with. Values can and do change based on our environment and the culture we're in.

We've known or heard of people with questionable family ties becoming good cops, committed to their community. We've also seen good cops turn away from strong values to unacceptable and even criminal behavior. No matter which direction people take, ultimately it's their values that determine their life path and their success or failure.

If you value service over crime, it's not likely you'll pursue a life of crime. If you have a heart (value) for service, chances are very good you'll end up in a helping profession like education, nursing, medicine, social work, firefighting, the military, or police work.

1.4 GUARDIAN VERSUS WARRIOR VALUES

A recent study by the *Police Executive Research Forum* found that law agencies spend an average of 131 hours training recruits on firearms, defensive tactics, and use of force scenarios, but only 26 hours learning communication skills, de-escalation, and crisis intervention.[49]

What does that say about what our profession values and believes is most important? You get what you focus on. Train and focus on force, you'll find plenty of opportunities to use your training. Focus on communication, de-escalation and crisis intervention and your officers will find more opportunities to employ those techniques.

We're not proposing to eliminate defensive tactics and use of force scenarios, but they shouldn't be a disproportionate part of your training. Instead, integrate all aspects of human interaction, communication, de-escalation, use of force and if appropriate rendering first aid, as one comprehensive training scenario. Instead of training in silos, combine all the disciplines into something that more closely resembles real life events.

Here's something many officers don't often think about: police actions regarding the use of force came under scrutiny long before the cases in the summer of 2020. The use of force has been a divisive issue since police departments were first created in the 1850s. We refer to the White House's final report on 21st Century Policing throughout this book. It's the best and most common-sense document on police reform to date.

It points out how the mission of law enforcement is "to build trust between citizens and their peace officers so that all components of a community are treating one another fairly and justly and are invested in maintaining public safety in an atmosphere of mutual respect." And it gives good information on how to do just that.

The task force saw procedural justice as the most important concept in its report. This concept is built on four central principles:

- Treating people with dignity and respect;
- Giving individuals "voice" during police encounters
- Being neutral and transparent in decision making
- Conveying trustworthy motives

Interestingly, the report says these principles of dignity and respect are both external and internal. That means they apply to our interactions with citizens in the community, and to the internal workings of the agency, and the interactions between colleagues and department leadership. The task force explained:

> Internal Procedural Justice tells us that officers who feel respected by their supervisors and peers are more likely to accept departmental policies,

understand decisions, and comply with them voluntarily. It follows that officers who feel respected by their organizations are more likely to bring this respect into their interactions with the people they serve.[50]

Researchers George Wood, Tom R. Tyler, and Andrew V. Papachristos from Northwestern University identified that distrust of the police is widespread and has consequences for public safety. They conducted a study to explore the consequences of implementing a procedural justice training within the Chicago Police Department (CPD) on filed complaints against officers, frequency of sustained or settled complaints, and use of force against civilians.

Results indicated that the one-day training (between January 2012 and March 2016) helped reduce filed complaints by 10 percent, frequency of sustained or settled complaints decreased by 15.5 percent, and use of force decreased by 6.4 percent. Two placebo tests were completed to help determine if any effect of training may have been the result of "time-varying confounding" (none were found). In addition, results indicated that the training continued to positively impact numbers two years post-study, implying the training had durability.

The procedural justice model "emphasizes transparency, explaining policing actions, and responding to community concerns." It incorporates "listening and responding to people in the community...and treating the public with dignity, courtesy, and respect." This being more productive and effective than many believe to be current day ways of policing- using "command and control techniques," dominating, and engaging in unjustified uses of force which provokes community members to feel 'demeaned, disrespected, and harassed" against. (Procedural justice training reduces police use of force and complaints against officers).[51]

That respect for the community and for the department goes back to—you guessed it—personal and agency values.

1.5 HOW AGENCY VALUES DETERMINE YOUR STRATEGY AND TACTICS

We've talked about personal values, now let's talk about departmental or agency values and how they determine your departmental strategy and tactics. Let's start with some basic definitions so we're on the same page there.

Strategic Definitions

- The strategic plan reaches down through the organization affecting and relying on contributions from every employee

- Vision is timeless, what we are striving to become in the ideal.

- Mission is our purpose.

- Values are our operating principles (Behaviors nest in the Values)

- Goals are long term (3-5 years) and refer to what the organization intends to accomplish over that time.

- Strategies are mid-range (1-2 years) and refer to how we will accomplish the goals we've set both long and short term. Some organizations refer to these as "initiatives."

- Tactics refer to what we can do today and tomorrow to achieve results. Tactics are specific, measurable, accountable, realistic and time specific (SMART). Some organizations refer to these as "action plans."

Before creating a strategic plan however, it's important to define your organization's core values. Your core values will dictate who you are, who you hire, why you hire them, who you promote, who you recognize for achievement and later, the elements of how your officers interact with one another and the community. These departmental values will also determine your branding, marketing and customer experience and eventually your departmental culture.

Creating Core Values

It's not impossible, but it is difficult to change someone's core values once they've become ingrained. That's why the military gets recruits while they're young before they've developed and solidified any undesirable values they may have. That's why they "break them down" and rebuild them, instilling the military's standards and values. They're trainable.

Honor, integrity, trust and similar values are instilled in military recruits from the first day they set foot in boot camp. There are recruits who don't integrate the values— but most do. The difference is values only work when you live them, not simply parrot them. The military understands values are critical, and we do too.

Everything that you're doing to get in your department, from values, morals, ethics, attitude, and people skills involves who you hire. Hire people who have the values you want, or hire people who can be trained to change their values to match your department's values.

Values are the key foundation for the set of competencies we have for our officers. If you go through the competencies we include, you'll see that every competency we require relates to an officer's values. The desirable state, the values we want to see are the values around caring for the people who are the recipients of the most police effort: everyone in our community, including the powerless, the homeless, the drug-addicted, the elderly, including those who break the law, in essence, any citizen who comes in contact with an officer for any reason.

We believe everyone should be treated with respect, as people with dignity and worth who matter no matter what situation they're in.

We treat people as people like we'd want our own family members to be treated. That standard, that ethos is woven into everything that we were already doing and it worked. It just got translated to the hiring process, to the performance appraisal process, and to the training process, through engagement with the City human resource department.

The public is already floating the idea of bringing social workers into policing. We go one better. We believe that it is possible to hire people that come in the door with the set of values that will foster things like empathy for others, strength to withstand scrutiny, courage and strong desire to help others. Officer Sean Payne suggested that on top of having a heart of service, you also want a person with a "teacher's heart." That's what we want, officers that can go the extra step and strive to be their best, when the rest of society is not doing so well. That's where our personality testing (such as Myers-Briggs), interview process, and how we hire for values and proficiency comes in.

We're not just hiring for Officer Friendly. We're hiring for what a community needs based on several factors, including the fact that police are responsible for public safety. There are instances when we need traits such as bravery in the face of danger for our SWAT teams and for that 0.5 percent of the time when truly evil people are seeking to harm others.

But more importantly, and above all else, we need smart, dedicated men and women that understand they are signing up for a dangerous job, one that requires them to think of the well-being of others, sometimes at their own risk. It is an amazing calling and they should always remember that only a handful of citizens are acknowledged as the guardians of our society, it is both a great honor and also a great responsibility.

Training is paramount to ensuring our officers apply measured restraint however ready to apply the traits of courage and bravery if needed.

More Community Input Needed

Sadly, when the police department or the city asks for input and engages people in focus groups or input through surveys, the people who respond to that call for input are the same people who have been responding for decades. They are typically people that have traditionally supported the police. Often they have a direct communication channel to city and police leaders.

Those responses to requests for input come from retirees, business owners, and the affluent, in some cases, they are community leaders that have adopted a philosophy of not pushing too hard on the police. There's nothing wrong with their input, or their experience and opinions—but it's not enough. More importantly, it's not representative of the majority of citizens who encounter the police on a daily or weekly basis.

Ramon's feeling is that supporters of law enforcement are at times restrained by their respect for the law and perhaps a sense on their part, that if they forced their message they would lose access. This was painful at times, because he genuinely felt that even when it was hard to hear others' criticism, it was his duty to interpret it and apply the best measures to address their concerns. The police and the government respond to citizens' questions with concrete answers—that's how it is supposed to work in a democracy.

Despite the challenges in impoverished communities, What gives us hope and the thing we find remarkable and heartening is that there's very strong support for the police and for public safety, from that silent, unpolled majority. It shows that despite the negative rhetoric, there are good officers out there doing their best and the folks living in those communities recognize their importance. What is key here is recognizing that there's a real need for more service, not less. Where we identified a gap in getting that support and feedback was in discussing how departments were going to reach those populations, and identify their values and needs.

If you hire officers with a mindset that sees the public as the potential "enemy," or "less than" or worse, if you allow a culture that accepts that sentiment, albeit unspoken, then your strategic plan will fail. Because values generally remain the same, they're the one part of your plan you can count on for decades to come. That's why it's important to get them right from the beginning and live by them! Things like:

- Treating everyone with dignity and respect
- Transparency
- Accountability
- Trust
- Authenticity

These values matter when you're determining your departmental values. Determine your values, then hire for those values.

Hire officers with a *guardian mindset*, that is, a defender, protector, or keeper and one who advocates for another, and you're more likely to find that officer has a "heart for service," not for violence. If you've been an officer for any amount of time, you know that not everything officers do is about protecting people. It's about serving and connecting with the disenfranchised of that community.. Every day, There are thousands of departments and police officers who extend a hand and "connect" with their communities in unexpected ways. The bridge between where we stand today and where the public wants us to be is not as far as some would have you believe.

1.6 IMPLEMENTING AND ENFORCING VALUES IN AGENCIES, COMMUNITIES, AND BUSINESSES

Do your personal values reflect the values of your community? Are they above the values of the community? Have you conducted focus groups, or asked citizens one-on-one what their core values are, not just what they wish they were? Have you met with the agencies who provide mental health or homeless outreach in your city or town?

Do you know what resources there are for battered women, rape victims, homeless families and runaway children? Do you know what their values are and which ones are in sync with yours? Do they know who to reach out to in the police department if they have questions? Do you have professional relationships with them? And most importantly, have you shared your values with them?

Does your agency make its values easy to find and understand? It's not enough to just post your values on a website. Department values should be clearly communicated to employees and the community, along with proof that the department takes adherence to those values seriously.

STEP 2: CREATE YOUR STRATEGIC PLAN

"Strategy without tactics is the slowest route to victory. Tactics without strategy is the noise before defeat."

— *Sun Tzu, The Art of War*

2.0 THE STRATEGIC PLAN: THE FOUNDATION OF A PERFORMANCE-ENHANCING CULTURE

This is the most important aspect of changing, reinforcing or achieving a higher level of performance for your organization. If you follow the process identified you will achieve results that are beyond your current state. This is not us making a wild claim. These principles are supported by research in publications such as *Good to Great* by Jim Collins and *Taking Performance Management to the Next Level* by Gregory Stoskopf.

2.1 WHAT IS A STRATEGIC PLAN?

One of the questions we get asked a lot is, what is a strategic plan? The next is, what is the difference between strategy and tactics? A **strategic plan** for any law enforcement agency provides, in writing, the vision, mission, values and goals of the organization over time, usually three to five years. It includes a detailed roadmap for how those visions and goals will be accomplished (tactics). A properly constructed strategic plan also provides stakeholders with the information they need to plan, budget, and pursue the priorities of the organization within the operating budget.

Strategy and tactics are both ways to achieve a goal. Essentially, *strategy describes your destination* and how you are going to get there, and *tactics describe the specific actions* you are going to take along the way.[52]

If your goal, for instance, is to have a department or agency with little to no complaints or incidents, and positive citizen response to your officers, your strategy is to create an agency with culture, values, a specific vision, and mission. The things you do to achieve that goal and pursue that strategy—your day-to-day action steps, the process, for soliciting broad community input, engaging the community in officer and PD interaction feedback, a customer survey, for holding officers accountable, your reporting and complaint process, your reward system, how you track incidents, complaints, etc., are your tactics.

All strategic plans are similar, but unique to their department. While you can use the report on 21st-Century Policing as a starting point or refer to the plans of others while creating your plan, you can't just adopt or copy a plan outright if you want it to succeed. Your strategic plan should contain goals, objectives, and projects personal and unique to your department and community. The one thing that every department can and should share is the five-step process we're setting forth in this book.

There are 900,000 officers serving approximately 18,000 law enforcement agencies across the US. Considering the different extremes of culture, size, goals, projects, and populations from each department, ask yourself, "Can there be a collective mindset, training, and strategy that encompasses every law enforcement officer from Miami to Alaska?"

Our answer is a definitive yes. All it takes is knowing how to turn great strategy into great performance. This is a proven process—not just something that looks good on paper. It works in real life, with real cops, in real departments, in actual cities and towns. It satisfies departmental goals and wins the support of communities and community leaders on both sides of the blue line.

2.2 POLICE AND A PERFORMANCE-ENHANCING CULTURE

For Mark, a performance-enhancing culture is very specific. It means having a strategic plan that includes connecting individual values with organizational values as we talked about in the prior chapter. Then it's about engaging everyone in the plan with specific tactics to accomplish. Next it's about measuring achievements while holding people accountable to meet their commitments. Finally, it's about reinforcing achievements. But, still, most importantly, developing a "performance enhancing culture" means starting with values.

EXERCISE 2: PERFORMANCE ENHANCING CULTURE SURVEY

For each of the following questions, assign the numerical score describing the culture of where your organization exists today. Assign the score for each question, then sum to the total.

- This is not important to our organization (1 point)
- At times we follow this descriptor and try to live by our understanding (2 points)
- Our vision, mission, values, and goals are framed on the wall (3 points)
- Our organization works on this with a clear timeline (4 points)
- This describes our organization today (5 points)

STRATEGY AND DIRECTION

We have completed an interactive process to identify our contributions to the organization.

Score_____

We have established our strategic priorities.

Score_____

We all know what successful outcomes or goals are for the organization.

Score_____

COMMUNICATIONS AND ALIGNMENT

We have clear metrics to identify whether we are on track in achieving our goals.

Score_____

Everyone knows how their work contributes to the success of the organization.

Score_____

The leadership meets on a regular basis to assess and make corrections to our plan.

Score_____

ACCOUNTABILITY AND COMMITMENT

Everyone receives regular feedback and we know how we are doing to achieve the plan.

Score_____

Our entire workforce is working to achieve the organization's success.

Score_____

Even in the face of setbacks we understand how we will get back on track to the plan.

Score_____

REWARDS AND RECOGNITION

We celebrate our success when we achieve our goals.

Score_____

We link success of the plan to our rewards and recognition.

Score_____

There are consequences for not working to achieve our plan.

Score_____

TOTAL_____

SCORING

48–60: Your organization has achieved a performance-enhancing culture.

36–47: Your organization is on track to developing a performance-enhancing culture.

24–35: Your organization has made some strides toward achieving a performance-enhancing culture.

12–23: Your organization has room for growth in developing a performance-enhancing culture.

A performance-enhancing culture comes from those personal values that fit hand-in-glove with an organizational culture that holds complementary values. For example, if you've got an "us against them" mentality where you don't trust, like, or even want to get to know the people in your community you're not going to enjoy working for a department whose number one value is community. The opposite is true. If you value community, help, service, and respect you're not going to do well in an organization that values intimidation and sees the community as a threat to their personal safety and well-being.

2.3 BREAKING DOWN THE FIVE-STEP PROCESS TO CREATING AND IMPLEMENTING A SUCCESSFUL STRATEGIC PLAN

The "five step process" is simple and easy to understand. However, depending on the values and culture of your department, and the organizational maturity of your department, it can also be a huge challenge to implement. No matter what, it's a powerhouse for change when followed. Here is the five-step process in a nutshell.

2.4 VALUES, MISSION, AND GOALS

Good, bad, indifferent or miscommunicated, all organizations have values—for good or bad. They exist. The challenges and problems departments, and you as chief face unfailingly fall back on those values, or a lack thereof. Think of the case where the values are on the wall but no one, including the chief lives by them or even knows them. Portland, Detroit, Seattle, Denver, Los Angeles, and

Miami have different community and departmental challenges than Bozeman, Montana; Johnson City, Tennessee, or Sitka, Alaska. However, the foundational issues that impact every department remain the same—organizational and personal values and the successful implementation of a well-designed and orchestrated strategic plan.

Every department, no matter its size or community challenges, needs to develop and successfully implement a well-articulated strategic plan. For their department to succeed as a law enforcement agency that plan must have built-in accountability, and measurements for evaluating the success of both performance and implementation.

That strategy needs to be based on the needs, values, culture, and policies of that agency. This means clearly articulated needs, and well-defined values and policies on both a personal (officer and staff) and organizational level. It's harder than it seems. This needs assessment may be from community forums, surveys , professional peer group reports, reports from recognized experts in criminal-justice reform, or department assessments. However, as we have mentioned earlier in this book, the key to understanding the "needs" is to listen to your officers, your department and the least "heard" community members. Those often disenfranchised and powerless community groups. Afterall they are the primary recipients of your services.

What we've found is that sometimes the *values* set by an organization differ from what employees and stakeholders or the community see. Sometimes organizational *behaviors* just don't align with what leaders say their values are. Sometimes those at the top of the hierarchy are disconnected and therefore have values that are not personally meaningful and are only advertised and touted, not lived.

Assumptions, individual beliefs, and personal values and views about professional expectations of those on the front lines can result in values moving and morphing into a culture the organization doesn't want with values among the ranks differing from values among leaders.

An example of this is if the leadership describes the organization as having a "Guardian" approach but an engrained, senior and respected group of commandeers, sergeants and officers secretly maintain a culture of fear and a "warrior mindset." Inevitably, if gone unchecked, or the source is not addressed, and/or changed, those beliefs will trickle into the culture, eventually resulting in undesired outcomes.

Without being redirected, these cognitive and behavioral ways of being can solidify, making directed change difficult. When "implicit values" and "explicit values" don't align, problems with "confusion, distrust, and cynicism" can surface.

Police Departments Are Powerfully Influenced by Their Values

According to DOJ experts Mark H. Moore and Robert Wasserman, the problem is that police departments, like many organizations, are guided by *implicit* values that are often at odds with *explicit* values. Explicit means something is made clear and stated plainly. Implicit means something is implied but not stated directly. Implicit values breed confusion, distrust, and cynicism rather than clarity, commitment, and high morale.[53]

For example, in terms of building internal trust, the command staff might espouse fairness in the execution of discipline (explicit), but their actions, shrouded in secrecy and viewed largely as unfair would be the implicit opposite of what they profess.

One of the more fascinating aspects about police values is that people generally get their view about those values from one or more of five sources:

- Hollywood and "police shows," either reality or drama
- Personal experience, usually through contact with police via accident, traffic, or other event (fire, natural disaster, burglary)
- Word of mouth from friends who experienced police firsthand
- Social media
- News reports and shared videos

For decades Hollywood and the police shows and movies never showed unnecessary police violence, and police departments considered movies and police shows and Hollywood as their own private public relations arm—until that suddenly stopped—thanks to television shows that began to portray police as incompetent, corrupt, and violent.[54]

About the same time the Hollywood narrative about police changed, the pendulum swung, YouTube and social media went from filming and posting real contacts with police to people actually creating opportunities to harass, film and display videos of cops being or reacting badly, even if they don't. The problem is, neither Hollywood nor YouTube presents a clear, realistic view of policing. And the statistics and facts that the Department of Justice, and others post, don't fit the narrative of social media or Hollywood.

Rightfully, every tragic outcome should be examined to better understand what happened and to mitigate the events from happening in the future (NIJ Sentinel Events Initiative) even when the probabilities of such events is a small sliver of a percentage compared to the number of contacts the police have with the public.

Unless you can create a department whose values, actions, integrity and goals are explicit, and have a community connection where citizens trust the department and its leadership and officers, you'll continue to battle mistrust and suspicion from your community and your stakeholders.

The media is quick to jump to judgement before the facts are in, and slow to follow up to correct mistakes. What we would like to see are more departments posting their values clearly and prominently on their websites so the public knows what to expect and what to hold a department accountable for.

Experience with a police department can be the byproduct of the policing style as policing style reflects a department's values. The two well-known police styles that Wasserman and Moore discussed were crime-fighting policing and community problem-solving policing. Both should have a place in your strategic plan.

What police departments experience are a lot like what any business experiences when it comes to "real values" and perceived values. A lesson learned: the owners of a large privately held company created what they called their "values." However, in working and talking to the employees, Mark discovered nobody in the rank and file understood what those company values were. They said, "Those guys (the owners) don't live by those values." There was a big disconnect between the owners and the employees.

What we did was go in and go through our values and behaviors exercise. We went to the different sites around the company and conducted focus groups where the employees would identify what their values were and then, asked for observable behaviors that supported those values.

From the behavioral data collected, Mark did a qualitative analysis and identified which behaviors were similar or the same, then grouped them as values. The employees identified a totally different set of values and behaviors than the owners had posted on the wall. Then he went back to the owners of the company and said, "These are the values of your company. They're not what you said they were, but what the employees said they were." The owners bought into it because they thought that the values that the employees came up with were better aligned with where the company was headed. When employees identify behaviors, values, strategies and tactics they have buy-in and from my experience will be more likely to achieve the results they identify.

It didn't surprise me that the values that the employees held were different were different from those of the owners. But what surprised me was that the owners so easily adopted the employee values. Often when employees are trying to speak truth to power, they are shut down or are ignored. But here is an example of a group of employees who spoke with powerful voices that resonated with the owners.

The same is true of law enforcement. It wasn't necessarily surprising when we found out that the values of the police department were closely aligned with what was already up on the bulletin boards at the department. But, again, it was surprising that employees often didn't know what the official police department values were, though they described their own values and those were closely aligned.

This story points out that if you have a command-and-control leadership in the police department that says, "Do it this way," and the employees or officers don't feel they have a stake in it, the changes or directive break down. That's why we thought it was so critical to let the employees have a voice in crafting the vision, mission, and values of a major city police department.

When Ramon first got there, he met with every employee unit in group settings. At the time, the comment he heard from the employees was, "No other chief has ever spent time to come and meet with us as individuals all the way down to this level."

It was a painful endeavor. It took a long time to listen to approximately 1,300 employees in small groups. Good or bad, Ramon took time to listen and understand what they all had to say. That was part of the whole experiment; to get their input and try to figure out where the common lines were that we could work off of.

At the same time, Ramon was thinking about the vision and goals for the organization with respect to how his own vision and goals aligned with those of the organization. Where's the alignment between the things that we were hearing them say, and what has been espoused for years prior to my arrival under their own values?

From there, we begin the process of pulling all of these things together. At the same time Ramon was also out and about in the community, listening to what the community wanted us to do. Our primary goal at the time was bringing all of these things together.

What did the community want? They wanted good police officers. They wanted good service. They wanted to be safe. They wanted to be treated fairly. Those things aren't out of the realm for what the employees thought that they were supposed to do. It was just a matter of fine-tuning those expectations so the community and the department were in sync. It was through Mark's and the leadership team's work that we put together that we were able to get this thing on the right track.

Three Foundational Challenges All Departments Face: Trust, Values, and Ethics

Let's start with the word trust. In *The Seven Habits*, Steven Covey had this to say about this foundational value: "Simply put, trust means confidence. The opposite of trust—distrust—is suspicion. When you trust people, you have confidence in them, their integrity, and their abilities. When you distrust people, you are suspicious of them, their integrity, their agenda, their capabilities, or their track record. It's that simple." [55]

Trust and ethics. We throw the words around a lot, but what do they mean? Where do they come from? Trust comes from our values. Our values determine our ethics. Our ethics determine our actions. Ethics are the moral principles that govern a person's behavior or how they conduct their actions and activity. Ethics evaluate those actions and the values that underlie them.

It determines which values should be pursued, and which shouldn't. Courage is one such value. Those who value courage are willing to stand up for what they believe, even in the face of strong condemnation, retaliation, or attack. Courage is a moral value when it deals with right and wrong conduct. Enough can't be written about the importance of courage in a police department.

"Trust produces increased speed, improved efficiency, and hence, decreases costs. Trust empowers ethical decision-making. Trust increases loyalty and the willingness to stay with a company. Trust decreases stress levels and hostility in the work environment."[56]

Here are the advantages of trust for a department:

- Trust builds morale, motivation, teamwork and collaboration.

- Trust overcomes resistance to change.

- Trust produces increased speed, improved efficiency, and hence, decreases departmental costs.

- Trust empowers ethical decision-making.

- Trust increases employee loyalty and an employee's willingness to stay with an organization.

- Trust decreases stress levels and hostility in the work environment.

- Trust breaks down corporate silos and isolating behaviors.

- Trust is a gateway to persuasion, sharing, and developing ideas.

- Trust is a key ingredient to coaching and improving employee performance.[57]

Whether you're a businessperson or a law enforcement agency, trust is essential to an effective team. Not only does it create a sense of safety, it creates an environment where employees feel comfortable to open up, take appropriate risks, and expose vulnerabilities.

Employees who trust each other will share knowledge with each other. A study published in the *Journal of Knowledge Management* found that trust was a key element in a team's knowledge acquisition. Simply put, if your team members trust one another, they're far more likely to share knowledge, and communicate openly.[58]

The first step in creating and developing trust is to Identify your department's values. The second step is to be able to put those values into your strategic plan. As we'll hammer home throughout this book, a strategic plan consists of your vision, your values, your mission, your goals, and how you're going to achieve those goals. Once you have a strategy then you create the tactics or day to day action steps you'll use to implement your strategy.

The third step is making sure everybody understands their role, and how they contribute.

The fourth step is implementation. Now that they've committed to something by putting it in writing and making it a part of the plan it needs to be acted on. You've got your concept, which are your measures and your metrics for the police department. That's the data-driven crime analysis you must deploy to try to figure out how to put what is called "cops on dots."

That's one of many crime fighting tactics, but it's certainly not the most complex. You're reporting on your tactics, which flow up to your strategy, which comes from your goal. That's the implementation phase.

The last phase is where you celebrate your successes to reinforce the change that you're making. This is a key part of the change process. In an organization that can pay for performance, that is the reward step. It's hard to reward others in police departments because you can't really use money to do that. You have to find other ways to reward people. Finding people-centered rewards—those intrinsic things that aren't cash rewards—has been proven to motivate people more than money.

Bestselling author, researcher, and head speech writer for former Vice President Al Gore Daniel Pink wrote *Drive*, an entire book on what motivates people. Pink argues that "human motivation is largely intrinsic, and that the aspects of this motivation can be divided into autonomy, mastery, and purpose."[59]

He argues against old models of motivation such as rewards and fear of punishment, dominated by extrinsic factors such as money. He writes that "based on studies done at MIT and other universities, higher pay and bonuses resulted in better performance ONLY if the task consisted of basic, mechanical skills. Money rewards worked for problems with a defined set of steps and a single answer. If the task involved cognitive skills, decision-making, creativity, or higher-order thinking, higher pay resulted in lower performance. As a supervisor, you should pay employees enough that they are not focused on meeting basic needs and feel that they are being paid fairly. If you don't pay people enough, they won't be motivated. Pink suggests that you should pay enough "to take the issue of money off the table."[60]

To motivate employees who work beyond basic, repetitive tasks, Pink argues that meeting employees needs in the following three areas will result in increased performance and satisfaction:

- Autonomy: The desire to be self-directed; it increases engagement over compliance.

- Mastery: The urge to get better skills.

- Purpose: The desire to do something that has meaning and is important. Businesses that only focus on profits without valuing purpose will end up with poor customer service and unhappy employees.[61]

Like Pink says, and we've personally observed, that what keeps us going is the direct acknowledgement that your part in the grand-scheme mattered—that our contributions were recognized.

Values

Place values ahead of profits. One corporate brand expert poses the question, "How do great companies create long-term success? Not by focusing on the balance sheet, but by improving people's lives based on strong, shared values using workplace culture. . . Values create the foundation of every successful organization. . . All the choices we make in life are influenced by what we value most."[62]

Honor and Integrity

Honor and integrity are the foundation of how we both operate. We genuinely feel that if we don't adopt and live these two values, then we won't have the ability to follow through on our commitments or keep promises. We also believe that eventually, not implementing and adhering to these two values, they will come back around—to bite you. In other words, you need these two important values to strengthen you and those with whom you work.

Ramon's Story

There are several definitions of what honor is. I believe honor involves living with a sense of respect for what you believe is right. Honor also means having great respect for yourself, other people, and the rules you live by. When someone is honorable, other people trust them to do what is right without having to watch over them to make sure they're doing what they've said they would do. Their word of honor means they will do exactly what they promise no matter what.

Honor isn't the glory, hero-in-the-spotlight kind of value. Rather it's about being "in the trenches, doing the stuff no one sees, or often never appreciates you doing" kind of character. It's also about having a core commitment to doing the right thing because it's the right thing, not because you're getting paid to do certain things, or because someone is watching.

Honorable people will do the right thing even if they're alone in a dark room. Honorable people do the right thing even if no one will ever know they did it because they answer to one person — themselves. It's a tough value to have, but because it's tough, and it's rare, it's all the more valuable to us.

Integrity is the character trait and quality of being honest and having strong moral principles; or a moral uprightness. A man or woman of integrity will also be a man or woman of honor. I don't think you can separate the two. Integrity shows up in the small acts; not gossiping, being honest in word and deed, not taking credit for things you didn't do or think of, not cheating on your spouse, keeping your promises even if you have to move heaven and earth to do so. Don't let someone else take the blame for something you did.

Follow company rules and procedures. Don't take shortcuts that will comprise or appear to compromise who you are and what you stand for. Own your mistakes. Be accountable for your own actions and decisions. Don't blame others for things you do, or choices you make. Be gracious. Be trustworthy, hardworking, helpful, patient, and responsible.

We've both seen public leaders that are missing honor and integrity and that, to me, has always been the greatest example of what I don't want to do and don't want to be. Part of that is about having honor and integrity.

The commitment to excellence and everything that I do, my character and being trustworthy and the competence to be able to have the skills and abilities to lead and to demonstrate how to do it right are what I value most.

Lastly, my family is so important to me. That's transcendent through the organizational family or, in this case as a police chief, the community as an extension of that family. Definitely, those are the pillars from where I operate and I always ground myself back to that.

When I was going through some of the hardest days of being a police chief, I would get up in the morning and I would start my day by thinking about the reasons why I was doing what I was doing. That *pause* I took each morning was the thing that kept me on course and brought me back to *why* I was committed to my vocation as a chief of police.

That energy and inspiration that you need to show up and keep going, especially when you're facing adversity, comes from having a core value of honor and integrity. You're doing the right thing and you're coming from the right place and you know it and that's what gets you through.

My honor and integrity values came to me from my grandfather, who had a lot of influence in the community and in our family. I thought he was very honorable and had a lot of integrity. He was always very committed and had a strong character. I grew up around him and he heavily influenced me.

In pursuing a career in law enforcement, it just seemed like what I viewed law enforcement to have, those types of values of honor, I wanted to be a part of that. I wanted to take my beliefs into an organization that I thought also had those same values.

With respect to family, my story is similar to Mark's in that I was raised by my grandparents, mostly as an only child. Later I joined my sisters and my mom around age ten. It was a really tough environment for me. My mom got divorced and had to work two to three jobs to keep things afloat. My dad didn't come through with his responsibilities. Those things also influenced my core values. I got to experience what it meant to be around someone who didn't come through with their responsibilities: my father; and to see what it felt like to be around someone who did: my mother.

Still, it made it a tough childhood growing up. I got a lot from seeing my mom work so hard. Watching her gave me the respect that I have for women now, and a firsthand knowledge of how tough they can be. The caring part of me for women is because I was raised around women. My sisters, my mom, my grandmother. But it wasn't until I got married that I was looking for a family unit that I could call my own, in that respect. Now I understand how important being part of a family structure and keeping that together is in the overall scheme of success.

Mark's Story

After honor and integrity, my values are strategic, excellence, continuous learning, health and family. When people develop values, those generally come from the family, culture, or faith. My values come from my family and the way I was raised. My parents died when I was an adult, so I didn't have that family to go back to. We don't have reunions or anything like that. My sister died, also.

Now, it's just me. When I married, I looked for a family unit. My wife's family was that unit for a long time. We're really close to all of our kids too. I talk to my kids (four boys ranging in age from 40 to 23) almost daily. I would say that my values come out of more of my experiences in life.

When it comes to learning about the values of others, I start with the leadership team. When I describe what a value is, it's something that we want to be known for. It links back to the story about "life is what we do between the birthdate and the death date listed on our headstone. That dash represents our lives."

What do we want to be known for when someone is giving a eulogy? What does our company want to be known for in the greater community after we're gone? What do we want to leave as the mark on our company?

That's how I get them talking about this. Then I have them brainstorm their values. I still am old school. I use flip charts and write everything on a flip chart and put them around the room. We might have 30 different values. Then I used a forced-choice method where I give every-body five dots (these are sticky, colored dots that we use for choice selection). I tell them to go around to these values and pick.

You can put them all on one or you can spread them out, but you only get five. You can't trade them back and forth. Everybody puts their dot with their selections up on various flip charts so all could easily see which ones the organization wants to be known for and you can get the prioritization of the values. When working with var-ious companies as I have, not just the police, if I didn't know there was a breakdown between the employees and management, I would still use the same technique. I would say, "We're going to ask the employees to define those values." How they would define those values and what are the behaviors that define the value. For integrity they would say things like:

- No BS
- Always be on time
- Be true to your word
- Do what is right even when no one is watching
- Deliver on your promises

Those would be done in a focus group setting. The medical company I referenced brought in 150 of their technical team in for a national conference. How do you have 150 people identify the behaviors that define the values? I had the whole 150 get up at twelve easel flip charts and did a round robin session where people move from one flip chart to another, everybody got to go to every easel. How else do you do this exercise with 150 people in an hour!

Ethics

There are core ethical values that all people should strive to achieve, such as honesty, kindness, compassion, respect, and personal responsibility. These are values to be admired and are illustrative of a person of integrity. The official Ethics Code for Law Enforcement Officers is specific, and detailed and says a lot about the value of integrity in ways any officer should be able to relate to:

The Law Enforcement Code of Ethics

As a law enforcement officer, my fundamental duty is to serve the community; to safeguard lives and property; to protect the innocent against deception, the weak against oppression or intimidation and the peaceful against violence or disorder; and to respect the constitutional rights of all to liberty, equality, and justice.

I will keep my private life unsullied as an example to all and will behave in a manner that does not bring discredit to me or to my agency. I will maintain courageous calm in the face of danger, scorn or ridicule; develop self-restraint; and be constantly mindful of the welfare of others. Honest in thought and deed both in my personal and official life, I will be exemplary in obeying the law and the regulations of my department. Whatever I see or hear of a confidential nature or that is confided to me in my official capacity will be kept ever secret unless revelation is necessary in the performance of my duty.

I will never act officiously or permit personal feelings, prejudices, political beliefs, aspirations, animosities or friendships to influence my decisions. With no compromise for crime and with relentless prosecution of criminals, I will enforce the law courteously and appropriately without fear or favor, malice or ill will, never employing unnecessary force or violence and never accepting gratuities.

I recognize the badge of my office as a symbol of public faith, and I accept it as a public trust to be held so long as I am true to the ethics of police service. I will never engage in acts of corruption or bribery, nor will I condone such acts by other police officers. I will cooperate with all legally authorized agencies and their representatives in the pursuit of justice.

I know that I alone am responsible for my own standard of professional performance and will take every reasonable opportunity to enhance and improve my level of knowledge and competence.

I will constantly strive to achieve these objectives and ideals, dedicating myself before God to my chosen profession: law enforcement.[63]

Brothers in Blue

We've both definitely seen family in the brotherhood of officers. It's like any other family; we can criticize each other internally, but to the outside we're a solid unit. There are moments of bickering and calling one another out when we miss the mark in our intention or outcomes. All of this can be healthy and lead to future growth and strength. But we must be mindful that the one aspect of family that is incongruent for law enforcement is that of public acceptance of criticism when things go wrong. As public servants first and foremost, our first allegiance is to our oath of office, the Constitution, the Bill of Rights, and the communities we serve.

Ramon's Story

As an assistant chief and later as a police chief I had the opportunity to attend executive training sessions around the country with other chiefs and assistant chiefs. I will never forget the story related to me by an up and coming deputy police chief (DC) in a major city police department. The DC had been observing his new chief and noticed that after a few months the chief had yet to talk about his vision, mission, goals or any of that. The DC told me that he tried to have a conversation with the new chief, but it never led to him understanding the new mission. The DC was eager and excited about new leadership and wanted to better understand the chief's long-range views, he respected his chief's experience and his position.

What the DC found out and what he conveyed to me was both understandable, but discouraging at the same time. The DC discerned that avoidance was a strategy on the chief's part. He was not trusting. He'd been a chief in another police department for many years. He had seen a lot of negative things and was purposely not showing his cards about what he wanted to do with the department because he wasn't sure if the people around him were going to be the right fit for the things he wanted to do.

He was holding back on telling anyone what he was thinking or what his plan was because he didn't want to get thwarted. Over time and through more experience in the executive ranks I came to see this exercise is a common occurrence.

It's like it's a defense mechanism or how a company or organization wants to move in a particular direction but doesn't really want to deal with the heartache of human beings being human in these situations, they are unsure and not trusting concepts they are unfamiliar with. Oftentimes a natural reaction to change or a perceived sense of loss within the dynamics of experiencing something new and foreign.

Mark's Story

I came up through the labor relations side of human resources. I really made my mark there. Through this path I received several promotions. One of the opportunities was for me to lead labor relations for Hughes Aircraft. Here I was able to get involved with the Federal Mediation and Conciliation Service. We worked together through an initiative called "Partners in Change" with our unions. The focus was on collaboration and cooperation noting that we were both in this together. As a result, we were able to make better changes faster with a "yes-and" versus "either-or" approach. Together in preparation for contract negotiations we jointly created a set of values by which we would conduct the contract negotiation.

When I was 40 I became the director of employee and organizational resources for Hughes Naval and Maritime Systems (NAMS). I was in charge of all the people processes: HR, security, facilities and property and everything that supported the success of the organization. I would sit down and meet with my boss, who was the president of NAMS, every Monday. I carried a yellow legal pad with all the telephone calls I had to make on one side and on the other side all the tasks I had to complete daily.

There were things like: fix this door, paint this wall, etc. I would sit down and go over my list with him. One morning he said, "Mark, let me see your list." I handed him my yellow pad. I was so proud of the list I had created. Then he surprised me. He nonchalantly took my legal pad, turned, and tossed it unceremoniously in the trash.

Then he looked me squarely in the eyes and said matter-of-factly, "Mark, that's not what I need you to focus on. I need you to spend your time figuring out how we can make this company a success and who we can make acquisitions that will help us grow. Then I want you, as our head of HR, to welcome the employees from the companies we acquire into our fold. Your goal is to communicate clear vision, mission and values. Then make the new employees feel a part of our company and then communicate succinctly where they nest -- where they fit. I also need you to offer a compelling story that paints a picture of our vision to all employees so that they know how they can help one another to become a stronger, unified company."

As I was young and not yet aware how to accomplish my boss's requests, I left that meeting confused and uncertain. I didn't know how to do what he was asking me to do. After I got back to my office I immediately called one of my best friends and I said, "I think I just got fired." He was a strategy guy. He responded calmly, "No. You didn't get fired. You just got handed the best job in the company. You now get to focus on fun stuff instead of the mundane day to day stuff."

The fact was it was time for me to learn the very important task of building a collaborative culture. What a great opportunity, this changed my life! You may now be or have been in a similar position to the one I was in—having to become a strategic leader who guides organizations through a process of achieving a shared vision. It's a very special job, well worth taking on.

I think that so many people grow into leadership positions because they're good at the tactical activities, but they don't know how to do the strategy. Hopefully knowing you're not alone in learning on the run will help you tackle your strategic plan. And, most importantly, realize you don't have to travel down this path alone. Take the time to get someone who can help you. It will continue to pay off again and again throughout your career.

Good Communication Breeds Trust

Developing good communications is a challenge for any organization but now more than ever before given the nature of our expanding virtual-centric world. Successful communication requires being able to connect intellectually as well as emotionally with a variety of people, cultures, values, and stakeholders. When building a police organization that operates optimally requires learning how to communicate *with* and *among*:

- Your officers
- Your superiors
- Members of the public
- City leaders
- Members of various media
- Your police union
- Local, state, and even national politicians

Leaders should be fluent in the language of various generations of employees/police officers in order to successfully engage them. When Ramon would go out and talk to communities of color, minority groups or others, he spoke unequivocally about the importance of making sure that in their interactions with police officers, they would treat the officers with respect and vice versa. At the same time he was trying to have conversations with the officers about always treating the community with respect, conveying an understanding of the challenges of dealing with people that are experiencing a mental crisis, under the influence of alcohol or drugs, people who may be having their worst day, that was when we had to be at our best. It's easy when everyone cooperates

He wanted to make sure that there was a voice for the officers. He spoke to communities across all sectors with the same message, that although constitutionally protected, they understood that the side of the road is not the best place to argue with a police officer. You don't get in a fight with an officer because you disagree with getting pulled over. He would tell people, "If you don't think it was done in a legal, lawful way or if the officer was rude to you, then make a complaint and I promise you—I promise you, you have my word—that your complaint will be looked at. Our officers wear body-worn cameras. We will review that and we will make sure that it is addressed. Don't start off by poking your finger in his chest and trying to get the best of him on the side of the road. *That's just never going to work out well.*"

Some of the things that keep officers going—and certainly one of the things that kept Ramon going—were the small events, the kind or positive interactions with members of the community where he thought, "It really is working." Every positive contact was more fuel for to keep going and it is the same for the officers on patrol. We're the police, but we're human beings. When you're exposed to so much negativity and criticism, it begins to wear you down. Even among all of that, you'd get one person that week that showed you kindness and appreciation and it was enough to propel you forward past the bureaucracy, the politics or the negative rhetoric.

Trust Breeds Success

Employees in high-trust organizations are more productive. They are also more satisfied with their jobs, put in greater discretionary effort, are less likely to search for new jobs, and even are healthier than those working in low-trust companies. Businesses that build trust among their customers are rewarded with greater loyalty and higher sales. And negotiators who build trust with each other are more likely to find value-creating deals.[64]

2.4 FOCUS ON CULTURE AND ALIGNMENT

There are a lot of definitions about what culture in an organization is. We see culture as groups of people, and the behavior, beliefs, values, and symbols that they accept and live. Unless exposed to value talk consistently—as in the military or law enforcement, etc. people, and groups tend to live their values without thinking about what they are, or why they matter. That creates culture and that culture is then passed along by communication and imitation. It's reinforced with every new hire and generally doesn't change unless acted upon by the leadership, or the hiring of a new wave of people with different values.

Culture is a system of values and beliefs which we share with our family, coworkers, or those we spend time with. Our culture gives us a sense of belonging or identity. Sports teams have a culture. Cops have a culture. Families have culture. We learn to juggle the various cultures, sometimes making life harder when those cultures clash and departmental values are ignored or substituted.

If you have a department with a lot of officers who value the community and keeping crime rates low, that's what your department will become—an agency with a guardian mindset and a heart for service. But if you have a significant number—or even a few people—with a mindset that sees that same community as a potential threat to the police, or as the enemy, your servant culture is going to be disrupted.

Studies have revealed that having just one person on a police team with a negative attitude and/or a checkered discipline history, has the potential to negatively affect all the good, well-intentioned members of the same squad[65] Just as in business, ask a patrol officer to tell you who drains the energy out of their team and they will not hesitate to describe them.

Some experts say there are two types of culture—material and non-material. Others say there are three, four, or five different types of culture. We believe the number of cultures doesn't matter as much as the type of culture.

Is your departmental culture aligned with your strategic plan, your community and the values of the chief and the department? If not, how will you bring it into alignment? Hint: it starts with the leadership.

2.5 DAY-TO-DAY ACTION STEPS

The day-to-day action plan is what set our plan apart from others in this arena. Accountability is baked into the system and the plan itself. Mark shares a great story about a private-sector company he worked with that lacked the follow-through to develop or execute a strategic plan. The CIO said they were too busy to focus on this work. The CFO said he didn't see any return on investment for the effort. And the head of business development said he had a better idea. It was never a cohesive team. They were always in their own worlds, not seeking the power of common ground and alignment. The CEO, who was new to the company, was enthusiastic but, sadly, he could not fight the old guard. They never accepted the opportunity to become a highly functioning team and unfortunately stuck to their old way of doing business.

Perhaps the lessons learned from that experience helped Mark develop the robust program to check and recheck our progress. His dedicated guidance and the assistance of a highly professional and very persistent Mesa team member specializing in project management were among the keys to our success.

STRATEGY MODEL

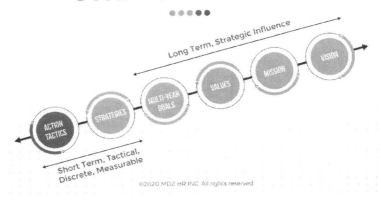

Long Term, Strategic Influence

VISION

MISSION

VALUES

MULTI-YEAR GOALS

STRATEGIES

ACTION TACTICS

Short Term, Tactical, Discrete, Measurable

Figure 2. Long-Term and Short-Term Aspects of Strategy

Define the vision, mission, and values

Your vision is the ideal version of what you are striving to become while your mission is your purpose. And then your values are your operating principles. These form the foundation of a performance enhancing culture, one that is aligned with the strategic direction of the accountable organization. Performance enhancing cultures are those that achieved the "good to great" as described in Jim Collins's foundational works, *Good to Great* and *Good to Great and the Social Sectors.* These works describe the results of organizations that follow this simple yet transformational model.

Develop an articulated strategic plan with goals and strategies to achieve your goals and SMART tactics.

This plan should include goals, strategies, and tactics, which are defined as follows:

- Goals are long term (three to five years) and refer to what the organization intends to accomplish over that time.
- Strategies are mid-range (one to two years) and refer to how we will accomplish the goals we've set both long and short term. Some organizations refer to these as "initiatives."
- Tactics refer to what we can do today and tomorrow to achieve results. Tactics are specific, measurable, accountable, realistic and time specific (SMART). Some organizations refer to these as "action plans."

We provide these definitions and encourage you to adopt formal definitions of the structure of your plan as we have learned from the work of Mankins & Steel, "Turning Great Strategy into Great Performance," organizations that don't speak the same language, in its most basic form, don't use a common nomenclature, cannot be in alignment. So a simple step to develop alignment is to use the definitions. Speak the same language.

Ensure that everyone understands they are accountable to deliver on strategic commitments

This means understanding and being accountable for tactics, deadlines, and deliverables. By utilizing SMART tactics and assigning them to individuals, not teams, you and the assignee will know what is deliverable, when and in what form. Remember the specific, measurable, accountable, realistic and time bound tactic creates accountability. We should also mention a very important concept, a team by its nature is not accountable, only an individual can be accountable. We often experience organizations that when learning the process of accountability, want to assign a tactic such as the selection of a new software to a team to get buy-in. Using a team to get buy-in is appropriate, but it's the ranking member or team leader who must be responsible for the work of the team.

There's a cartoon where someone asks "Who is responsible for this?" and everyone on the team points to someone else. Don't let this happen, assign a tactic to an individual.

Measure performance to the plan

It sounds simple, but you can't measure what you don't understand. Create a process or a tracking tool to incorporate the goals, strategies and tactics. Ensure that you have a regular process for review of the plan. A great way to ensure tracking of the plan is to implement a strategic council. A strategic council is the body that is responsible for ensuring the accountability of the plan.

The best way to describe this group is to look at the charter of another council established to lead, oversee, and guide the strategic planning of the University of Arizona Honors College:

> The University of Arizona Honors College Strategic Council comprises the leadership of the college: the Dean; the department managers; representative faculty and staff members; and key stakeholder representatives. These key leaders provide direct linkage to the UA at large, stakeholders, community, staff and students; to ensure communications, transparency, alignment and commitment to the Honors College strategic plan.

> The charter of the strategy council is to adopt, initiate, influence, make adjustments to and champion the Honors College strategic plan; and ensure alignment with the stakeholders, partners and University strategic plans. The council will meet at least quarterly to report on and monitor progress toward achieving strategic goals and to resolve accountability, resource and priority issues.

The council will consider recommendations on implementing and/or discontinuing strategies, tactics or activities. The council will make strategic decisions on resource allocation, identify and resolve funding requirements and prioritize strategic initiatives. The council will review progress to the plan and accountability of participants. The council shall develop and deliver communications on plan activity.[66]

You also need a formal process or system with dashboards so that visually you can at a glance review and monitor organizational progress to the plan. Any time you can visualize the data in such a way that everybody in the room can see what's up and what's down and what's worked and what's still in process just at a glance without really needing to work at it is phenomenal for the team.

Additionally, you must understand the plan and the goals, not just know what they are. Do you see how everything works together? If you can explain it to a peer or other staffer, you do.

Recognize and reward strategic achievement

Depending on your style, culture and values rewarding people for essentially "doing their jobs," can be hard. Instead of seeing rewarding people for doing their jobs well, see rewards as something you do to mark or recognize reaching a goal, helping the department achieve a strategic mile marker or accomplish a critical achievement.

Here we are shifting to talk about police related examples. In this instance, every agency or department is different, but all strategic plans will include specific departmental goals, such as, but not limited to:

- Reduce crime

- Reduce or eliminate citizen complaints about, or use of excessive force

- Reduce injuries or fatal accidents

- Provide exceptional customer service at every police engagement

- Strengthen community partnership and communication

- Increase use and effectiveness of technology in the department

- Promote and encourage employee health and wellness programs

- Increase and strengthen competencies

You can't accomplish any goal without having and implementing the most critical aspect of any goal—personal and departmental values. We repeat this often throughout the book because it's so important.

Discovering and establishing organization or departmental values from the beginning is the foundation for creating any strategic plan. You can't have one without the other. By having an articulated strategic plan any department, regardless of size, culture, or location, can create a department that consistently, over time minimizes force complaints or incidents; builds strong community support, and continues to mature professionally as an agency.

Defining the Policing Problem

A great deal of the value of any strategic plan is lost in its translation. For whatever reason, no matter what the distance from the top of the department to the bottom is, the best of plans aren't making it to the people who need it most: the employees, officers, the public, the politicians and the unions.

Performance issues and bottlenecks are often invisible to senior management, which leads to frustration among the rank and file. The public, city officials and politicians also misunderstand, or never hear about the chief's plan— or don't grasp its importance. This strategy-to-performance gap not only causes confusion, but also results in or fosters a culture of severe underperformance throughout the organization. Organizations typically realize only 60 percent of their strategies' potential value because of defects and breakdowns in planning and implementation, and communication.

To avoid this problem, we've developed a strategy and implementation system where:

Strategic planning and implementation are inextricably linked.

- CEO or chief raises the bar for both planning and implementation.
- Leaders continuously monitor performance.
- Leaders hold themselves and others accountable.

Our strategic plan solution isn't rocket science. It's actually quite simple, clean, and doable no matter what the size of your department, or your culture, or what your resources or budget is. Among the solutions we teach:

- **Keep your strategy simple.** Everyone in the department should understand it and be able to repeat it and explain it if ever called upon by the public or the organization to do so.

- **Make it concrete.** Don't wander off into the stuff of public relations fluff. It needs to be clean, simple, and solid.

- **Use a rigorous framework, speak a common language.**

- **Clearly identify priorities.** Not everyone has the same priorities as you do. Make sure you communicate clearly about priorities and the reasons or process by which those priorities exist. It might be budget, or culture, or diversity.

- **Continuously monitor performance.** When people know their performance is being monitored and evaluated in order to help them perform better, they respond more consistently.

- **Develop implementation capabilities and reward performance.** Remember it's not you. It's your staff who must implement the plan. It's up to you to hire, develop and promote the best talent to achieve the desired outcomes aligned with your values. Ensure that you have the right people and they are assigned to the right strategies. Then with each success recognize and reinforce the achievements of the plan.

There's more we'll discuss in the following chapters. What we hope you'll understand from this book is that a department with a minimum of complaints and incidents of use of force *is definitely* possible. The support of the community for the police, for police training and funding, and a police presence is also entirely possible.

Best of all, satisfied, loyal officers, and a community lower in overall crime, violence, and community engagement are within reach of any department.

STEP 3: ENGAGE EVERYONE SO THEY KNOW HOW TO ACHIEVE THE PLAN

3.1 CHANGE MANAGEMENT, CULTURE, AND COMPETENCIES (THE SECRET SAUCE)

Change Management—the people side of change—is the most critical and difficult aspect of change. Managing the people side of any organizational transformation will always be the most challenging, and rewarding, part of any change you implement. The second most challenging aspect of change management is to change culture. You can't just get people to change. You must find a way to change the culture they operate in, know, understand, and embrace. You need their buy-in which can come from inclusion, knowledge sharing, transparency, and most of all building trust among those going through the process of change. If your organization's culture isn't aligned with your strategic plan and your proposed structure, your changes won't take. It will just confuse you and your team.

Crafting goals, setting timelines and deadlines, and creating budgets is the easy part. As we stated before, spreadsheets don't get emotional, feel threatened, or need to defend their turf. Goals are straightforward and deadlines... well, calendars don't need to feel important or respected. People do. Not everyone is good at managing people.

You can be an officer's officer on the streets, but dealing with employees, stakeholders, politicians, and supervisors—the heart of change management—is the most challenging job you'll ever have.

If you have 20 officers performing a task, they will approach that task in 20 different ways with 20 different reasons, justifications, ideas, and skills. Most of them will get to where you want to go, but it's rare they'll all take the same path to get there.

They may follow the same policies and structure, but each approach will be unique. As a leader you must not only understand that, but also manage each one as needed. Some will need more direction, others less. Some you'll need to walk through a process step-by-step. Others will be able to take a three-sentence explanation and deliver a perfectly crafted project, on time or early, exactly as you envisioned it.

It's all a part of change management. Each of them must understand..."what's in it for me?" Once they know, understand and accept it they will join in and often become your change champions. As difficult as managing people through changes can be, managing major culture shifts is even harder. Think a magnitude of ten times more difficult.

We're telling you this not to discourage you, but to give you a heads up about what to expect. Cultural change can be managed—with planning and certain tactics.

Mark was certified in 2019 in change management. You wouldn't even think there was such a field as change management , but there is. He needed to learn change management because he knew it would provide a critical skill we would need to show departments how to deploy their strategic plan. Some important things to know about effective change are:

Begin by assessing and defining your current cultural values. You can't change what you can't measure, and that applies to culture and values. By knowing what your current culture is and what values people have, you can determine how much (if any) change is needed. Getting a baseline for the existing culture will give you a starting point. You'll know where change is needed and how to approach a culture change.

Understanding your department's current culture will enable you to intentionally realign it with your strategic plan. When we say "culture," we mean everything from job descriptions, job competencies, personal and departmental responsibilities, performance appraisals, your reward of compensation and pay structures, promotions, and training. These should all be aligned like a set of gears and operate as a system as each impacts the other.

Ensure staff and stakeholder participation. You can't make meaningful, lasting, or critical change without the support of your staff and stakeholders. Whether you use meetings, exercises, retreats or regular talks, make sure you have the support from key players. Don't think you can get their attention or cooperation once and then just forget about it. Ensuring consistent support means frequent, consistent, relentless and redundant communication about the personal and cultural changes the department is/will be undergoing, the benefits everyone will receive, and what you anticipate the future being and bringing.

Use posters, video, exercises, metaphor, stories, words, actions and reminders to keep your message upfront. Remember the success of storytelling from the New Zealand Attitudes and Values Study referenced in a previous chapter? Those learnings can be applied here. Long after you've tired of the message, keep repeating it. People will need to hear, see, and experience the change much more frequently than you think. It takes most people 30-45 days of daily focus to change one small habit. Imagine how much more it takes to change an entire culture.

Manage the emotional responses. Your employees, staff, and stakeholders aren't the only ones who are going to feel emotional about change. You will too. It's important that you pay attention to your emotions and model them to communicate positive reactions to the change.

According to Wharton's Executive Leadership Management, "Leadership effectiveness in times of change has been found to be critically related to the use of emotional intelligence. Employee emotions have a strong influence on how they approach change, and leaders need to be as analytical and strategize as much about their emotional messages as their cognitive ones."[67]

Further, the above study references the importance of paying attention to your employees' emotions and talking with them about their feelings and thoughts regarding changes. Be empathetic and patient. Personal and cultural changes come with anxiety, anger, frustration, doubt, and resistance. It's natural. Don't take it personally. Learn how to manage the extremes and support your staff and employees through the changes. Expect to fall back two steps when you advance one step. When we wait, taking two steps back for every step forward, we'll never get anywhere. No matter what, be aware of your own emotions and always role model the change you are trying to create—both emotionally and cognitively.[68]

Focus on Competencies—The Secret Sauce to Effective Change

Competencies are the "secret sauce" to success in a properly designed and implemented strategic plan. Imagine hiring someone without knowing what their job skills are, let alone not knowing what skills the job you're hiring for actually demands. That's where competencies come in. They are the structure holding your organizational gears in place.

Competencies are the behaviors that demonstrate the knowledge, skills, abilities and personal attributes that distinguish superior performers from their peers. We created, then incorporated very specific competencies into our strategic plan.

Our Strategic Initiative: Workforce Planning & Employee Development – Actions to build competencies for all levels of the organization, including a time frame and end date for achieving these competencies:

- Patrol officer
- Sergeant
- Lieutenant/professional manager

While knowledge, skills, abilities, values, and personal attributes all underlie a person's behavior, their behavior is all we can see. A competency-model is utilized to identify the visual behaviors and achievements that distinguish high performers from average performers.

Our strategic plan with Mesa began in 2019, and extended to 2025. Our primary objective was to get full buy-in from the police officers, sergeants, lieutenants and commanders to embrace the competency plan.

When the concept of competencies was put into the strategic plan, there was a group of commanders who led a team that came up with a concept of mentoring and engaging the workforce in identifying what their needs were by asking them what they needed, and then creating mentoring opportunities for them. One of the great things that came out of that initiative was the idea of incorporating and mentoring to competencies in the organization. This was a first step in buy-in.

We asked questions like when do we know that somebody is performing the way we want our top performers to perform and what does it look like from a behavioral standpoint? And what is the performance at the highest level? Most often it was the workforce itself that correctly identified the ideal competencies.

To answer those questions, what we did was develop a small team to go out and participate in ride-alongs with officers, conduct phone and face-to-fact interviews with officers. We then ran focus groups with the officers and the sergeants, and then presented the information to the commanders to also get their input. Then we wrote up our findings and delivered them.

We came up with ten different competencies— everything from customer focus to use of technology. We identified behaviors that the highest-level performers would demonstrate. Those were what we might call "champions." Those were the highest-level performers. Then we had the "meets expectations" group – what behaviors they would demonstrate and then what "needs improvement" behaviors were.

We went back to that same group plus spent a lot of time with the training group. We understood how their training fit with implementing the competencies. We verified whether those behaviors that were listed in each competency were indicative of those three levels of performance across those ten different competencies.

It was interesting to find out that the officers really embraced this and really took it to heart. It just so happened that one of the people who was on our consulting team, was a PhD candidate at Williams James College in Boston. She coincidentally worked with a Boston area police department on mental health and drug addiction issues. What she did for us was provide insight into the social issues that officers face. We incorporated social, substance abuse, homelessness and mental health issues into every competency, at every level. We included what engagement with that segment of the community would look like, what caring would look like. Those got incorporated into every one of the Patrol Officer 2025 competencies.

Between doing the training at the academy, and using those competencies to recruit police officers, we saw a difference. Additionally, we used those competencies to train the new recruits and the current officers. The field-training officers use these competencies to measure and reinforce those behaviors in their students. They then tied that back to the performance review system. With recognition and reinforcement, those behaviors would start to materialize.

We said that by 2025 we wanted these to be our standard. We knew it wasn't something we were just implementing for the short term. We knew it was going to take time and would be a cultural change. All the competencies were tied back to the values. This is how it ties into the strategic planning and the values.

We did research on where this was done. It was occurring in Europe, Canada, and California. We used a model from Sacramento and Toronto combined. For patrol officers, we had competencies that included:

- Adaptability and decisiveness
- Trustworthy
- Initiative and perseverance
- Interpersonal skills
- Judgment/problem solving
- Learning, memory and recall
- Organizational skills
- Stress management
- Valuing service and diversity
- Verbal and written communication skills

These were in a big matrix. Each competency had definitions. Each competency also had the behaviors associated with each definition clearly outlined. It was definitely all about enhancing a culture that never abandoned its roots of public safety while leveraging their strength and belief systems around the principles of engaging and embracing our community.

During the planning process we also shared the competencies we were working on with the city because the city was partially responsible for recruiting. They were also responsible for the job descriptions, the performance review process and the compensation process.

Both the city HR and our department team were so excited about these that, together, we created new systems to deploy the competencies. The department team figured out how they were going to incorporate the competencies into the new training at the academy and how they were going to take the competencies and put those into the field training assessment. It was a great win to get the city to buy off on the competencies and allow us to implement them into the evaluation process. That was huge. There were many people in the HR department, but we only met with two. Those two might have said, "Okay, we'll do this," but to implement it took maybe a dozen people – all the way from the Assistant City Manager who has responsibility for HR all the way down to the IT specialist who ensures that it's on the internal drives. In a way, we were celebrating what we had accomplished.

Duty and Responsibilities

Police officers, as part of the law enforcement system, have four major responsibilities:

- Enforcing laws
- Preventing crimes
- Responding to emergencies
- Providing support services

We propose, however, that the above four are just the baseline for police responsibilities. Further we advocate for inviting police officers and their departments to move to the next level of growth where the following three responsibilities, if embraced, can lead to better outcomes:

- Adaptability and trustworthiness
- Memory and recall
- Value in service diversity

These are just as, if not more important. It's much easier to take a community-oriented approach that deters, prevents and supports citizens rather than just arresting and prosecuting them.

Think of it as what is called the "broken windows theory." The broken windows theory is a criminological theory that states that visible signs of crime, literally, broken windows and antisocial behavior, and civil disorder create an urban environment that encourages further crime and disorder, including serious crimes. "Broken windows," is both a literal term as well as a metaphor for disorder within neighborhoods. Ramon met George Kelling, who helped devise the theory. He said it wasn't all about crime fighting and arrests, it was also about repairing the windows.

Like many things, at the earliest time, the concepts of the article took off in one direction, focusing on crime and missing the opportunity to fix and remediate the broken buildings that created the opportunity for crime to occur. In order for the reform era of policing and criminal justice to take hold, our country, our local communities have to address the glaring societal issues that for years, have been laid to rest on the shoulders of the police. Asking the police to mitigate all crime is akin to asking a hospital to cure a pandemic. We wouldn't think of it in those terms because we realize the enormity of it all, the same goes for crime and policing.

Disorder and incivility within a community are linked to subsequent occurrences of serious crime. By fixing or preventing broken windows, both literal and social in neighborhoods, crime and disorder are reduced. By responding to emergencies, offering community support and programs, and preventing crimes and appropriately addressing those that break the law, a community is strengthened and crime reduced as well.

This broken windows theory begins with hiring people who have a deep commitment for service and sacrifice. Officers and staff who are empowered by their leaders and committed to support their neighborhood and practice community-oriented policing, with a culture of service is where successful strategic planning begins.

3.2 COMPETENCIES AS A SYSTEM

UNIVERSAL COMPETENCY MODEL
● ● ● ● ●
THE VALUE OF COMPETENCIES

CLASSIFICATION, REWARD AND RECOGNITION
Competencies give employers clear definitions of job duties, responsibilities and metrics used to classification and salary structures.

PERFORMANCE ASSESSMENT
Competencies become performance metrics. Employees know them ahead of time, work to develop towards competency growth and improving perceptions of procedural justice.

COMPETENCY

TRAINING AND DEVELOPMENT
Curriculum can be designed around desired competencies. Links employee development to clear competency outcomes.

LEADERSHIP, CAREER AND ENGAGEMENT
Competencies can be used to ensure employees understand how they contribute and identify individuals to fill specific positions and/or identify gaps in key competency areas.

RECRUITMENT AND SELECTION
Behavioral event interviewing, increasing the validity and reliability of selection, promotion decisions & organizational fit.

Figure 3. The Competency Star

As mentioned, the competencies operate as a system. As a set of gears that mesh perfectly with one another and transfer the power of the strategic plan to the organization through your people. These are the people systems of your organization. The competency star (Figure 3) describes how the people systems are as impacted and supported by the competencies.

EXERCISE 3

Consider your organization from a people process stand-point, how do the 5 points of the Competency Star work together in your organization? Start by giving a score between 1-5, five being the best for your current performance level at each point of the star. Add your scores. A score of 21-25 indicates that your people organization operates as a system, you are Exceptional and can teach others something about competencies and people processes. A score of 15-20 indicates that you are performing as meets expectations for a well-functioning organization. You still have room for growth. A score of 14 or less is a good indicator that you have a developmental opportunity. Read on.

We created competencies for all job levels: patrol officers, sergeants, and lieutenant and professional management competencies. Competencies consist of behaviors, abilities, knowledge and a mindset that establishes expectations of specific duties, assignments, roles and expertise in a set of readily identifiable behavioral examples.

PATROL OFFICER COMPETENCIES

- Adaptability/decisiveness
- Trustworthiness
- Initiative/perseverance
- Interpersonal skills
- Judgment and problem solving
- Learning, memory, and recall
- Organization skills
- Stress management
- Valuing service and diversity
- Verbal and written communications skills

SERGEANT COMPETENCIES

- Professionalism
- Trustworthiness
- Taking initiative
- Conflict management
- Judgment and problem solving
- Supervision and leadership
- Identification with the organization's mission and values

LIEUTENANT AND PROFESSIONAL MANAGEMENT COMPETENCIES

- Accountability
- Trustworthiness
- Taking initiative
- Conflict management
- Judgment and problem solving
- Professionalism
- Identification with mission and the organization
- Management and Leadership

Those are the competencies we want to see, and these are how we define and evaluate them. Below, for instance, is *just* the accountability competency. We created definitions for each competency in each job designation or level. Contact us for more information on the competencies at www.donoharmbook.org. Every department requires different competencies related to their strategic plan and their department values, size, and other considerations.

ACCOUNTABILITY COMPETENCY

Being responsible and answerable for one's own actions and those of subordinates. Ability and confidence to vary between being flexible and holding firm on a decision, depending on what the situation requires; showing leadership by adjusting one's approach to the demands of a particular task by taking and maintaining a position in a self-assured manner.

EXCEPTIONAL

- Accepts ownership of own actions and the actions of subordinates
- Holds self and others accountable for mistakes and related results
- Is courageous with addressing concerns with higher levels of authority
- Works effectively in ambiguous situations
- Consistently keeps staff informed of projects and status
- Consistently meets with staff to discuss their projects and status
- Learns from past mistakes and ensures they don't happen again
- Seeks out feedback and makes behavioral changes based on it

MEETS EXPECTATIONS

- Takes responsibility for mistakes of self and others
- Sets expectations and holds staff to them
- Keeps promises and agreements
- Takes action when needed
- Focuses on issues at hand as well as clientele
- Accepts feedback and makes behavioral changes
- Makes good decisions based on the situation at hand

NEEDS DEVELOPMENT

- Calls out those who make mistakes
- Blames others for decisions, even if decision was their own
- Does not address employee bad behavior
- Makes excuses for situations or items that have been mishandled
- Does not take timely action
- Is stoic
- Does not administer consequences when needed

NOT OBSERVED

- Competency not demonstrated or observed

These are simple examples; more detailed and specific behavioral examples would need to be developed for your organization.

The competencies were a game changer for everyone at every level. People now knew what was expected, what was demanded, and how it was measured. Through the celebration of the small wins, the team could envision the future, and see how everyone was pulling in the same direction. There was a joint feeling of accomplishment and success as they worked toward the same ends. Also, competition was against their own performance, not each other. Everyone had something to strive for individually as well as by being part of something bigger than themselves.

3.3 COMMUNICATION FROM THE TOP DOWN: DEALING WITH DISSENTERS AND RESISTORS

Anyone who has ever been in charge of anything at any time in their lives will agree that leaders will encounter three kinds of people — those who are onboard, excited and proactive; those who cooperate because they trust the leadership, even if they're not overly enthusiastic followers, and then there are the resistors and dissenters.

Resistors come in all flavors, ages, genders, and backgrounds. We've found personality indicators, like the Myers-Briggs assessment , are a huge help in understanding individual style and through that understanding, why and how the resistance exists. A staffer's personality type, their employment history, status among their peers, and other factors, including any control issues, are a good place to start. The employee's perception of what is happening, and what they expect based on what they know, or have heard, or believe (true or factual or not), also affect resistance.

Any control or perceived control in an area, can also trigger resistance. Either of those can throw up roadblocks simply because there is a particular feeling people have when they experience a loss of control. It doesn't mean there is a loss, only that the employee believes there is. This can be frustrating for leaders and employees alike.

Resistors and dissenters aren't necessarily bad people. They're people focused on what's in it for them, or how a change will affect them personally. They resist because the change threatens or scares them in some way. As a leader it's your job to understand the reason(s) for the dissent or resistance and address it or them.

If you're a leader you have to be cognizant and proactive to recognize these preemptively. You need to think about what roadblocks a directive might inadvertently create. So you have to create a vision of what the future-state looks like. Sometimes even then people won't go along with the program.

Here's the main thing to remember about resistors: People do not resist change they believe is in their best interests. They resist because there's something about the change they believe, suspect, or feel is not in their best interest.

For instance, when police body cameras first came out in 2009 many officers thought the cameras would be harmful for them. Many feared the cameras would interfere with an officer's ability to do their jobs without worrying about being second-guessed or "Monday morning quarterbacked" by supervisors, other officers, or even the public who would be watching the videos.

There was resistance and a lot of grumbling about being "forced" to wear them. Concerns of privacy and the consequences of "being caught on camera" rippled through police departments across the country. In the small town of Rialto, California — one of the first departments to use cameras, Cpl. Gary Cunningham, an old-school cop, admitted he thought the cameras would be used to punish officers. Then the data and the numbers came back.

In 2012, in the first twelve months of the pilot program in Rialto, with half of the department's 54 uniformed patrol officers wearing cameras, complaints against the police dropped 90 percent compared with the previous twelve months.[69] In a three-year post-experiment, another study found these results remained stable.[70] The Rialto Police Department had been reeling from a series of abuse scandals before the cameras.

Use of force by officers fell by almost 50 percent over the same period. Suddenly, in a job where all complaints against police were a matter of "he said, she said," and angry accusations and lies about what happened, there was proof that the body cameras were protecting officers—not harming them.

The grumbling eventually subsided and officers who initially resisted the cameras embraced the technology once they realized the change really was in their best interest. These results were not unique just to Rialto. Departments all across the country were finding the cameras were showing police doing their jobs correctly.

The camera footage not only resulted in higher convictions, but also showed officers doing courageous things such as pulling people out of burning cars, or rescuing suffocating or choking citizens. Cameras captured officers and citizens at their best as well as in their worst moments. Unlike what most officers had feared, the cameras proved to be closer to being a cop's best friend than their worst enemy.

Perception and anticipation impact employees' responses. This is true whether the change is in patrolling, reporting, processing, or daily procedures.

Reasoning with resistors and dissenters rarely works, but understanding why they are resisting or dissenting and then addressing that concern, does. In 2018, Ramon attended a conference hosted by the Police Executive Research Forum (PERF), where chiefs from across the country heard firsthand from young police officers from different jurisdictions as they described their experiences with body-worn cameras. The officers were unanimous in their support and belief that body-worn cameras are tools that protect everyone. One officer said he couldn't imagine going to work without it. The body cameras are viewed as a way to level the field, instead of solely relying on edited cell phone camera video, the officers have their own undisputable, full-length account of all incidents.

Mark's wife is an instructor at the university in Tucson. There are ongoing conversations about what's happening with COVID-19 and reopening up the campus. Faculty members disagree about how to proceed. The business school, the college of public health, and the college of sciences have are doing research and writing research papers. These are widely published and have supporters and detractors.

Mark argued that at some point the president of the university has to stop listening to all the dissenters. The dissenters in this case are the faculty groups, the graduate student group, and different groups that don't necessarily contribute to the success or progress of the issue. What they do is create a lot of negative dialogue that impedes any forward progress.

His wife argued that the president has to listen to the dissenters, because if you find just one nugget of information from one of them, then you've advanced your mission significantly. That nugget she was talking about is almost always the thing the dissenter believes is not in their best interest. Once again she was right!

Resistance and dissent are rarely irrational. They have valid points we need to consider. Even serial resistors and dissenters will change if they decide the change is in their best interest. It's all about communications and understanding.

3.4 WHAT CAUSES RESISTANCE

Some people resist because they enjoy it. It's part of who they are, their character or personality style, or "it's their thing." Fortunately, they're in the minority. We know most of the reasons people resist or dissent, which is half the battle to dealing with that resistance.

The Five Areas of Resistance

1. **Analytical:** The analysis of paralysis. You never get to do something because you get *stuck* thinking about what needs to be done but not moving forward and ticking off the milestones to get to the finish line.

2. **We've done this before**: Many will say or think something like "It's a waste of my precious time." But I'm sure you've seen plenty of organizations that have one or more of their past strategic plans sitting on their office shelf.

3. **Too busy:** We're too busy and mired down by the tactical. We can't possibly do something strategic. Alternatively, we don't want to do the strategic because that means more work for us.

4. **I'm just not interested in doing this.** This is the passive aggressive person. They may not ever say they're not interested, but their behavior demonstrates that they're not interested.

5. **I'm no longer in control.** This is perhaps the primary reason for resistance. All resistance stems from some internal feeling, perception, or actual loss of control or loss of ownership of a particular area that they've invested in. The reasons given above may be the first ones that come up, but at the root of resistance, conscious or unconscious, is the fear of losing control.

We believe that one of the things in any change effort that can't be underestimated is the inherent ownership that people in an organization have over established norms. Any disruption or any perceived threat of disruption to that ownership or that feeling of control over a particular area of expertise, can trigger the reactions that sometimes come about such as those we just brought up, above.

So, for any leader considering implementing a plan as we undertook, you have to be cognizant and cautious that you will need to be ready to address these issues. We guarantee you, issues will abound. With so many different officers with so many diverse personalities, challenges, levels of maturity and experience it will become necessary to be responsive and incredibly patient and flexible. It's important to recognize the people that you're working with and to see and try to pick out, preemptively, where some of those roadblocks may occur.

Be proactive. If you know someone is highly invested in their position, address their fears as soon as possible.

You've got to be able to tell them what's in it for them. Know that even if you do that and more, that sometimes folks will still not go along. It's challenging but worthwhile, always, to pursue.

3.5 DEALING WITH AND RESOLVING RESISTANCE

Mark learned the best process for dealing with resistance in any endeavor from a Prosci training session. First off, resistance is one of the most difficult things that we have to overcome in implementing a new strategy. We've listed many of the reasons why people resist, but here are the top ten ways to deal with that resistance:

Listen and Understand the Objections

A critical step in managing change is to listen to the objections and understand what the resistors are really objecting to, not just what they say they object to. What can you do to eliminate the objection? Going back to the body camera issue, one of the officers' biggest objections was being second-guessed after the fact.

What they really objected to was being held accountable and having to change their usual approach to community encounters.

Focus on the What, Not the How

For some types of change it's important to let go of the how and focus on what needs to change. Often employees will already have ideas on what needs to change. Listen to their ideas on how to change. The people on the front lines every day often have better, more effective ideas than those with little exposure to the challenges.

Remove Barriers

Barriers to change, feedback, or suggestions, or even direct orders to follow a new policy may relate to a person's family, personal issues, politics, or cultural limitations or money. By fully understanding the barriers or perceived barriers and determining ways to address and resolve or avoid those barriers you can avoid a lot of stress, misunderstandings, and more pushback or dissent. Removing barriers means active listening and hearing what a person says, or doesn't say, in order to understand what the barrier is. An officer who suddenly resists working a certain shift may have child-care issues they didn't have before.

Provide Simple Clear Choices and Consequences

Don't be a "helicopter leader," meaning don't hover and micromanage your employees. Trust them to make good decisions. Be clear about the choices people have and make the choices simple. "If this, then that," kinds of choices are often helpful.

Communicate in simple terms what the choices and consequences of each choice are. If an officer or staff member needs more training to make good choices and decisions, give them the training. But, let them make the choice. Empower your people to make those choices. It not only re-enforces their values, it helps them mature, grow and trust you more as well.

When given the opportunity, training, and support to learn how to make good choices, most people will do so. They'll also tend to resist less because they have more control over situations they're responsible for.

Create Hope

Many people respond to the opportunity to create a better future for themselves, their colleagues, and their families and community. Leaders can create excitement around such opportunities by sharing their own passion for the change/future.

Show Real and Tangible Benefits

You can't determine whether change is good or not without a baseline or comparison. Seeing is believing, and facts and proof demonstrate the benefits of change through the use of case studies or pilot programs. Don't just institute change without measuring the existing program first so you have something to compare it to.

Make a Personal Appeal

These work best with established open and honest relationships, "I believe you and I share the same values about , but that we just differ on how to go about achieving the same end. Can you trust me on this and will you go along with me on this this time?" When we are open and honest with people, including staff, employees and even superiors, we may step on toes or offend, but ultimately our honesty, and the trust we have built, will help us move past what might otherwise be a deal breaker or sticking point. This means you've got to keep depositing social credits in your relationship accounts. You can't keep making "withdrawals" without putting credits into the relationships. Reciprocity, not money, is the thing that makes the world go around.

Convert the Strongest Dissenters

Groups follow their leaders. It's true among officers as well as sports teams. It's true for men and women. It's true in the C-suite culture of CEOs and managers, as well as among blue-collar workers. Followers will rarely buck the natural leader and step outside the culture. They may buck an appointed leader if they don't respect or trust them, but natural leaders lead because the group trusts them.

That's why when you convert the leaders, or your strongest dissenters, the rest of the group converts as well. Your original dissenters often become your most vocal allies when you show them how change favors them. Leaders stay in power by taking care of their followers. When you can point out how a change can secure their power, provide for their followers, and enhance their leadership, most will revert and go along with the change.

Demonstrate Consequences

Not every dissenter is willing or able to recognize how change benefits them or their followers. If you can't convert a leading resistor or dissenter, your only other option is to remove them, or eliminate their power. Often removing a key individual who is demonstrating resistance is a powerful signal to the rest of the organization. You send the very powerful message — "We are serious about this change and about doing what it takes to implement it."

Provide Incentives

Focus on a critical few people, natural leaders, or those committed to the change. Focus on who can make a difference if they lead the change. Increase their compensation or provide another incentive that is directly correlated with the success of the change. The incentive may be more power or control, greater visibility, or a promotion. Look at the personality and what motivates those leaders to determine what incentive will work best. For some, it's an award ceremony and recognition of their peers. Others prefer a promotion, a bonus, or more time off. Make sure the incentive matches the person's motivators.

3.6 HOW PERFORMANCE GAPS CRIPPLE GOOD ORGANIZATIONS

The "performance gap," as we call it, is that no-man's land between departmental success and stagnation. On one side is our strategy, on the other is our goal, but without a system or plan to get from one to the other, our strategy might as well not exist at all.

It's like the 80/20 rule. Eighty percent of the population goes along with and engages with you. You've got 10 percent that is the challenging/questioning group and then you have another 10 percent that they're not going to go along with you no matter what you do. They're just out to sabotage the process. When faced with these 10 percent resistors using the ten steps identified above, engage each individual and convert one resistor at a time.

We believe that if you understand the groups that you have and act on the premise that change occurs one person at a time, you can change the entire group. However, don't attempt to take that whole group and try to change that whole group all at once. That will always fail!

Pick one thing that's occurring from that group and address that. If you've got 100 people that have that issue, if you deal with that issue and you change one person at a time, the others will bring people along.

Going back to dealing with resistors, the same dynamic and tactic is true for many changes. Find one person, a natural leader who the group already listens to and respects. They are someone who can become the sponsor or the champion of the change. Get them on board and they will basically change the entire group.

The way many departments approach strategic planning is basically the same. The department or agency holds some focus groups and has a facilitator come in and write down all the things that people want to do. Then they bring those project suggestions back to a leadership group. That leadership group identifies a half a dozen or eight areas that they want to focus on.

Those goals are typically aligned with the way the organization is set up. There are rarely any surprises. Basically, every leader has some kind of a goal in his or her area.

Once they have those goals they put them into a nice glossy chart that they hang on the wall. Then they say, "This is our strategic plan. This is where we're going and this is our five-year plan." They may not understand what a strategic plan is, what it should look like, or what elements it needs. They're just told to "copy" an existing plan from some other department or business.

For example, Mark took one sheriff department client to lunch and we talked about strategic planning. He said, "Yeah, we've got our strategic plan and I've been told to make it look like Los Angeles Police Department's (LAPD) strategic plan and to prepare a document that we can send out to the community and say that this is our strategic plan." He gave me a copy of the LAPD plan. It was a good-looking, glossy document. The problem was, there was no accountability in the plan. There may have been accountability, but that was not covered in the glossy plan.

The gap occurs in the difference or the variation from what leadership publishes and says they're going to do versus what the employees look at, believe and say about it, "That's all a bunch of BS. That's just a document that we send out to the community. We do it every three or four years and it goes away."

This particular client asked for help in replicating that plan for his organization. Mark said he couldn't do that because the document did not represent what the department was actually going to do. It was not done with integrity.

With regard to Mesa, the three bureau chiefs took their projects, initiatives, and ideas, and put it all into a three-ring binder. These were submitted as the strategic plan. That's where the eighty-six initiatives and more were recorded. These documents were given to two of us to resolve. In situations like this, where we have multiple projects, we take another approach. Eighty-six is too many projects for any organization to tackle.

At Mesa we were fortunate to have a very talented staff member who organized, sequenced, and assigned reasonable timelines on what she referred to as this "portfolio of projects." She identified the project management tools and processes to schedule the projects within the portfolio so that they would be logically sequenced. She ensured that the money we were spending on the projects could be projected and tracked.

From a project management standpoint, what we did was cluster together those things that were similar. Then took them back to the strategic council, which was about twelve people: the six bureau chiefs, the chief, the lawyer, the CFO, and others who were involved in running the department to rank, prioritize, sequence and take ownership.

To get this done, we used a forced choice exercise where each person is given five sticky paper dots. They had to go around the room where each project was posted on a large chart and place their dot to identify their top five projects.

They thought it didn't give them enough input. It only gave them maybe eight projects that they could all agree on that they needed to do. Was eight projects enough? Was it within department resources and budget? Those became the highest-priority projects. Through additional discussion and prioritization they identified 22 projects that they wanted to do, which is still a lot, but many fewer than the original 86—and still within budget and department resources. This is how a well-functioning team sets priorities, shares resources, and identifies their strategic focus.

Those projects fell into about a few goal areas. You can see how we were able to do four things here:

- We reduced the number of projects to a manageable amount by having the stakeholders, the chiefs, and others determine the priorities with a forced choice methodology with brightly colored dots.

- We eliminated the gap between what the employees were saying they wanted to do and what the leadership had initially said they wanted to do by taking those top twenty-two projects and going out to the workforce. The workforce, including the patrol officers, now had a chance to say what was important to them.

- Once we had the workforce feedback we came back to the chiefs and we said, "Here is the ranking of projects that your people have identified." That's how we closed the gap.

- Then we identified the costs of all of these projects to see what we could afford. Once that budget was identified, we figured out the cost of each one and then the chiefs prioritized those. They knew they needed more money, but now they had a chance to prioritize the projects.

For example, in another law-enforcement organization, one of the top officer priorities was to refurbish the gym, physical fitness and endurance facilities. The track was rutted and potholed, the equipment was held together with silver duct tape, the mats were worn and generally the facilities were in worse condition than the city parks.

In that case, what that strategic council had to do was go back and find funding that they could then refurbish the facilities, fix the track and provide new, safe equipment because it was such a high priority for the officers. Funding was identified in the following year and this became a follow-on initiative. The strategic council agreed with the officers' priorities.

At that point, we had our top initiatives, we had the cost identified, we had the people involved identified. Most importantly, we identified and listed the timelines, deliverables, and accountabilities of those people responsible.

If there was to be a team, we identified the leader and put that team under the person who was responsible. We then wove those accountabilities into a big project plan, the strategic plan. Every month, we would come back to meet with a strategic council. The team leader would present progress, barriers, obstacles and accomplishments and identify if resources were adequate to accomplish the tasks assigned. To my astonishment, it was rare that a leader asked for additional resources and if he/she did it was reasonable and justified. The strategic council concept worked.

We all know what happens when you "finalize" a plan. Something happens that throws a wrench in it. Sure enough, a major project came up after we had already identified and finalized the plan.

Many of the recommendations now had to fit into the plan, be measured, and have somebody assigned to them. But that was okay. Having your plans change last minute doesn't have to be an issue. The key is not in how many changes, activities, or projects. The key is in having an oversight body that understands the total complexity of the plan and somebody assigned to each initiative or activity to accountably shepherd the project.

As long as you have someone who is responsible for doing the follow-up and reporting back to the strategic counsel on its implementation every month, it works out. Every month Ramon sat with the strategic council and reviewed every one of those twenty-two projects. He looked at the progress, the barriers and the completion, whether they needed more money or if they needed more people on the project. He reminded them that these were *their* priorities and this was *their* strategic plan. The plan progressed on track, on schedule and on budget.

We didn't need to publish a glossy document. We just needed to be able to be accountable to the city council, the city manager, our community and ourselves on what we were actually doing.

The key was Ramon's leadership and his enrolling his leadership team on a different way to do the strategic planning. Although Ramon is gone, they still are following that strategic plan and following that process of meeting once a month and reporting on the status of the plan. At the end of the first year, we went back through and we found that there were eight initiatives that were completed. We added another six back.

It was those sixty-six others that sat out there. They hadn't made "the cut," but they weren't forgotten. On a long-term plan, you can't do everything at once. You've got to prioritize and do what's most important, where you have energy and what you have money for right now.

Get those top priority things done and then, as more money comes in, a new budget year arrives or you finish projects, then you determine what the next group of projects will be based on your priorities.

STEP 4:
HOW DEPARTMENTAL
COMPETENCIES FIT INTO
STRATEGY

4.1 DEFINING PERFORMANCE STANDARDS

How do you define your department's performance standards? Recognize first what they are. According to the Office of Performance Management (OPM) a performance standard is a "management-approved expression of the performance threshold(s), requirement(s), or expectation(s) that must be met to be appraised at a particular level of performance."

In other words, that means performance standards are the establishment of organizational or system standards. They are not based on individual performance. They're the targets, and goals you set to improve and standardize the accepted level of performance by an employee on the job. They are based on the position, not the individual.

Performance standards can be set on national, state, or legal guidelines, benchmarked against similar organizations, the public's or leaders' expectations, or other methods.

4.2 IMPLEMENTING THE STRATEGIC PLAN

Many agencies create what they believe is a strategic plan — often on the fly, or based on existing information or initiatives or linked more to marketing and branding the department than running it. They don't build in accountability, day-to-day-action-plans, or deadlines and reviews. Then they say, "Strategic plans don't work." There are lots of reasons they fail and almost all of them have to do with two things: they aren't true plans, or they are improperly implemented.

A true plan, properly and consistently implemented, will work most of the time. If it fails, it's time to pinpoint why it failed, then correct it and launch again. Most of the time failed plans are due to superficial planning or preparation. This is not a project you can throw together in a month.

Complete the Full Plan

What you should know about strategic plans that no one ever tells you:

A well-defined strategic plan doesn't come together in a day, a week, or even a month. The time you need to develop a plan varies on the maturity, size, and dynamics of the organization. Plan on no less than three to four months to create and develop your plan. You can't rush it. Take the time you need to get it right.

You can't create a robust, working plan without input from your stakeholders—not just the obvious and historic stakeholders, but the members of your community who don't get to weigh in on how your plan will impact or affect them—the homeless, the single moms, the mentally ill, the social workers and medical community need to be heard too.

You can't just have people write their ideas down and submit them. You can start your research that way, but the more time you spend actually listening to people — and we mean actively focused listening — the better your plan will be. A lot is lost in translation from a scribbled note to a face-to-face meeting.

Whenever possible use a facilitator to help people get their ideas out. Not everyone you talk with is going to be a skilled communicator. But they may have insightful ideas and observations you can use. It just takes a skilled communicator and/or facilitator to pull that information out.

There are many great techniques available now where you can use a smartphone to gather information and do voting and forced choice. If that's not an internal skill it's worth having a consultant coming in to run focus groups for you and get it done just as quickly as possible.

For instance, at Mesa PD, once we got people's input, the project portfolio manager and I sat down and interviewed everyone who had submitted an idea. Sometimes we would have Ramon's leadership team join us, people would come in and talk to us and present ideas to us, and sometimes Ramon would sit down with members in key positions in order to better understand their view and their challenges to implementing the plans. If this sounds labor and time intensive, good observation—it is both. But worth it!

Anything worth having or doing takes time and this is one of those things. The more you put into the process, the more you're going to get out of it. Yes, it's long, sometimes boring or repetitive, and it will tax your patience at times. That's normal. Keep moving forward. Don't let your eagerness to reach completion get in the way of your success. Maybe it will take a year or more to get this input if you're actually going out into the community. Remember, the input is valuable but your time listening and engaging the community may yield your greatest returns.

Once you have all your projects, initiatives, and ideas, begin to think in terms of "sequential planning" and timelines. Sequential planning is critical because you can't do all the projects/initiatives all at once.

Sequential planning means your projects and initiatives follow a logical order or sequence, or to have a working plan. Before you can have city-wide patrols you need police cars and trained officers. Before you can have a bike patrol you need bikes, then you need officers who can ride them, are trained to deal with the unique aspects of bike patrols and community, and who are physically able to spend a day on a bike — that sort of thing. And, your planning has to be sequential. Which comes first? The bike patrol training, or the bikes, or recruiting for bike patrol officers?

Be aware of both your personnel and financial resources. Each is a constraint and opportunity. Make sure you have enough of each.

Timelines mean not everything everyone wants is going to be possible in the first year, or even the first three years.

You Are Not Santa Claus

What creating a strategic plan (especially in the social services sector), most people get the board and leadership to do the planning, and list the projects or initiatives they'd like to see. This is somewhat similar to telling kids Santa will bring them anything for Christmas that they can think of in ten minutes. When you ask people what they want/need for their department or staff, they're going to come up with a whole bunch of projects—and most of them are going to be wants, not needs.

It's akin to "let's throw everything against the wall and see what sticks." Not much will stick, and even if it does, it doesn't mean it should have. What most people do when they create a strategic plan, is to get the organization's board and leadership to do the planning and list the projects or initiatives they'd like to see.

Regardless of what does "stick," most projects will not be put into the first 12 months of the plan. Because this is a project focused plan. You should focus on a needs-based plan. It's rarely financially or reasonably possible to serve all the individuals. Trying to force the plan results in failure, overspending, and a variety of other issues.

Anything that gets pushed out beyond 12 months is going to disappoint, anger, annoy, or send the unintended and personal feeling message that their project isn't "important." If they understand and are engaged in the process they will help set priorities, understand the resources available and champion the final plan.

It's important to preface and explain the strategic planning process so everyone involved has both an understanding of the process, and gets to have input so they have skin in the game and buy in. Remember our "sticky dots voting" exercise?

This allowed people to have some control over what initiatives were approved and prioritized without one person controlling the decisions. This way you're not the "bad guy" saying "no" to everything, and people have accountability, control, and a sense that their project is important because they participated in the prioritization.

They're also more likely to accept the scheduling since it's determined in such a way that it makes logical sense in terms of sequence and budget.

Wish List Versus Strategic Plan

Many people confuse initiatives and planning in general with what a strategic plan is. What occurred when we received those 86 different initiatives was that we learned some of them were things that people had wanted for years, but those requests had been turned down again and again for whatever reason. What the police heard was, "Share with us everything on your wish list," rather than, "Let's start with a strategic plan that focuses on those things that are most important currently and will make the most positive impact on our mission."

This prompted people and departments to take the items they wanted (wish list) and add them to a very fast-growing list of initiatives, even though their choices had nothing to do with the strategy or helping the organization move forward.

There were also those who wanted to relieve themselves of certain activities or obligations. To this end, they tried making some of their desires, strategic goals. But in review, we saw some of these requests as clear misalignments of delivering the best service possible. It took a lot of work for those involved in the planning process to ensure that every goal tied back to the values they chose.

The possibility of divesting responsibilities that were not in alignment with the strategy was something that came up a couple of times during our planning process and implementation.

If there was misalignment, we still had opportunities to discuss them with the executive leadership team and make quick determinations as to how to course correct so everyone stayed on track in order to achieve the goals and vision they created.

Vision, Values, Missions, and Goals

Your vision for the strategic plan is not your lone vision. It's a collection and amalgamation of everything you learned during the information gathering phase. That means the more productive your interviews with the community, with stakeholders, with officers, and with the typically disenfranchised populations as well, the better your plan will be.

If you can seek out and find those community members who rarely get to have input into these sorts of documents, all the better. This means the homeless population, the social service workers and agencies who work with the mentally ill, and those community pockets of poverty as well as local hospitals, doctors, and anyone who works with the population your department is likely to see or engage with. This additional effort on your part increases buy-in and builds a coalition of champions across your entire community in support of your department and the plan.

As you prepare, and begin to develop your strategic plan, keep in mind your mission, and goals as well. Where do you see yourself, the department, and the community in one year? Two? Five? By knowing what your goals and mission are, based on community, stakeholder and employee feedback, you can reverse engineer what it will take to achieve those goals. If you envision a community wide bike patrol of officers, and all you have is a newsletter from the International Police Mountain Bike Association (IPMBA), you're going to need to find out how to get from point A—where you are now with nothing, to Point Z—a fully functioning, viable, and valuable patrol of bicycle officers.

Let's use this bike example to understand the structure of the strategic plan (refer back to Figure 2). From that graphic we'll demonstrate the goal, strategy & tactics. In this case the goal could be to engage the community to advance mutual respect. The strategy is community-wide police department bike patrol.

Then there are many actions or tactics to achieve the strategy. Some tactics could be:

- Engage the community through forums to identify the priorities of patrolling.
- Identify how the bike patrol will be equipped.

- Develop the plan to select officers to be assigned to this patrol.
- Understand the criteria to determine the effectiveness of the bike patrol.

Following is a simple example, note how that three levels are directly related to one another and that the tactics include actions to engage, implement and measure effectiveness.

Day-to-Day Action Steps—Tactics

Your strategic plan is more than a vision for the future. It's a plan for today, tomorrow, and all the day-to-day strategic activities your staff and officers will encounter to achieve the department's goals and mission. It's a living, breathing plan. When one thing is accomplished, based on your established priorities another moves in to take its place in order to allow the next item to be addressed. It's a system, where one action logically and sequentially follows another.

Many have heard of SMART goals. We use the term SMART tactics: S (specific), M (measurable), A (accountable), R (realistic), and T (time-bound). Tactics are simply the day-to-day steps you and your organization take to remain accountable to the strategic plan.

Most of us already do this thought process in our head - automatically. If you don't, or you or your employees struggle to get things done day-to-day, this action list process from PeopleAssistant.com or Mindtools.com contains good, basic explanations or examples on how to create day-to-day action plans.[71] Following are three things you should do to make the most of your action steps:

One: Identify SMART Tactics

What tasks do you need to complete to accomplish your strategy? Using the SMART Tactics model, what do you need to do first? Once you've accomplished that, what's next? Do you need to delegate or get other people's projects done before you can tend to yours?

It's helpful to start this process at the very beginning. What's the very first action you'll need to take? Once that task is complete, what comes next? Are there any steps that should be prioritized to meet specific deadlines, or because of limits on other people's availability? What's your deadline? Is there a deadline?

Two: Analyze and Delegate Tasks as Necessary

Once you've seen, then broken down the task into steps, look again. Can you drop any of those steps and still meet your objective? What can you delegate? Do you need additional resources? What tasks have deadlines, which don't?

Three: Double-Check With SCHEMES

- S (space)
- C (cash)

- H (helpers)
- E (equipment)
- M (materials)
- E (expertise)
- S (systems)

You may not need this entire list for most action items. Take what you need and ignore the rest. Following this process works well for most mid-level to advanced tasks.

4.3 GAINING COMMUNITY, OFFICER, AND STAKEHOLDER SUPPORT

Here's the one simple rule and the secret to gaining community, officer, and stakeholder support: clear, frequent communication, feedback, and follow-through with everyone involved in your changes.

At the beginning of a change initiative, developing a stakeholder map could help add clarity as to who the stakeholders are, their relationships, their importance to project success, analyzing their level of support can help with project success.[72] Stakeholder involvement can help provide strength, support, and resources for a project's successful completion or a lack of involvement can mean the demise of a project or change initiative.[73]

Establish an open dialogue from the beginning of any plan, any changes, or the implementation (or considered implementation) of your plan and continue to communicate even after the change is complete. It sounds redundant, or even easy, but it's not.

That's because people don't always hear your message. They hear what they think you said, what someone else said you said, and what they remember hearing from the last time someone talked about change. That means you have to repeat yourself numerous times, always with patience; because if you say it with any hint of anything else, your tone changes the message.

If you don't think communication is important, consider this: a survey by *The Harvard Business Review* found the average realized performance out of a strategic plan is 63 percent. That 37 percent loss is made up of about ten items, with number one being communication, translation, or understanding.

If you have an administrator who has never worked a street beat, it makes it hard for them to understand, or communicate with those who do. That's the primary reason strategic plans fail—there's a failure to communicate or translate what needs to be accomplished

So, begin communicating changes internally and regularly, *before* you take it to the community or the media. Get your patrol officers, sergeants, and leaders onboard first. Let your stakeholders know. Your messages should be consistent across the board.

Don't just communicate your changes, but communicate the reasons for the changes. Explanations about your thought process, the board, and anyone else on the leadership team are critical. Explaining your reasons can increase understanding and prevent people from feeling threatened.

Remember, the number one reason people resist and dissent is they feel, imagine, or believe the change(s) that are coming will negatively impact them. By eliminating those fears right away, you save yourself a lot of stress. This means your communications, especially oral communications, must be carefully thought out and your speaking points memorized. Other tips:

- Don't try to dump everything on your department at once. If you have been engaging the department and community from the beginning there will; be no surprises. Start with three items, then add more as people become comfortable and adjust to those changes. Not everyone will comprehend the details in a talk. Make sure your speaking points and the changes are made available through the interdepartmental website, a memo, email, a poster in the locker room, at roll call, the breakroom, or where employees tend to gather as well as in a staff or employee email, remember to engage your internal audience with the same energy and passion that you do with the community, they deserve no less!

- Remind yourself that a strategic plan is a marathon, not a sprint. As exciting as goals, strategies, tactics, and change can be, you can't maintain that initial level of excitement and still maintain the organization and its normal tactical duties.

- Encourage positive discussion about the changes, but be open to questions and constructive criticism as well.

- Remind people the department doesn't have the money to implement all of those things you want to do — but that the Strategic Council or you've prioritized projects according to budget. Give them a view of the big picture. The overall picture was great, but we had to put it into bite-sized chunks so that we could measure it, and manage it.

- Celebrate wins all along the way. These celebrations, no matter how small, are the fuel that feeds the successful implementation of your strategic plan.

As the leader of an organization, and one that wanted to see change happen, Ramon was looking at a lot of aspects that needed to be tackled. But he had to temper his excitement. He didn't want to overload the system. There were many great ideas about how to begin to move the organization forward, but at the same time he had to balance ambition with reality. He wanted to focus on those areas where they could leverage gain, and mark off some wins to celebrate.

By celebrating wins at strategic points they could build the momentum to keep things moving in the right direction and keep members' enthusiasm up about the fact that a positive movement is happening.

He was fortunate: the executive team was filled with great talent and many more were literally waiting in the wings—commanders, lieutenants, and professional staff who were ready to take on the next challenge. They were leveraging the enthusiasm of the people who were implementing the plan and it was working.

4.4 MEASURE PERFORMANCE AGAINST THE PLAN

Most social service organizations track their performance by metrics such as budget, membership growth, number of visitors, people served, and overhead costs. These metrics are certainly important, but they may not measure the real success of an organization in achieving its mission. By linking metrics in the strategic plan to your mission, you will be focusing on both what your organization envisions and what your customer expects. For example, if you have a goal involving community engagement, then your strategies and tactics should result in a metric that measures community engagement in support of your goal and the mission. It's all aligned from tactic up to vision and from vision down to the tactic's details (refer back to Figure 2).

You can't change what you can't measure. Data alone is worthless. Data *analyzed* reveals patterns. Patterns tell stories. Stories educate, teach, and prepare the way for change. Create a baseline for performance before you implement new performance requirements. What are the standards your patrol officers and sergeants are measured against now? What are the new standards? How much time do they have to learn the new standards and then change to meet them?

In order for police departments to shift their focus to outcomes,[74] tools that evaluate their communities' feedback are not just desirable, but mandatory. Feedback shared via subjective encounters from people on the receiving end of police services can provide measurements of ways to shift the delivery of services when appropriate to reach better outcomes, such as the reduction of crime as well as the continued cultivation of trust by the public.

These performance guidelines must include a high level of interactivity with a department's internal dynamics. This will be directly reflected in the efficacy of the police when it comes to addressing crime rates and victimization, the creation and development of public areas that are safe, and doing everything possible to enhance the overall quality of life in the community.

Stakeholders in all levels of the police force must be fully onboard and living the values and mission of the agency. Community policing, full-service policing, will require that every member of the organization understand that they are a component of what makes it work, everyone plays a role. The philosophy of full-service policing in the twenty-first century has to be ingrained in the fabric of the agency.

Recruit and hire the right people. Then follow with thorough training with high standards is necessary to foster this result, and vigilance for the maintenance of this must be employed through proper oversight, leadership and management so that all members uphold the mission and values in their everyday living so as to avoid the loss of community support and cooperation, and that the organization's reputation remains unharmed.

Traditionally, police have tended to utilize surveys to measure public sentiment in their communities. However, surveys are expensive and time-consuming and typically wind up providing data that is insufficient when it comes to gauging the results of police intervention or public events within communities.

The good news is that with today's advanced big data mining solutions, in-depth sentiment analysis within the private sector can create a viable feedback loop that helps high-level decision-makers have a better comprehension of those public feelings as well as identifying potential risks. In this twenty-first century climate of policing, it's wise and in fact, necessary, to gather and integrate this type of information into police performance management. Moreover, leaders should be transparent with their findings, internally and externally.

Those of us in policing must be willing to embrace this type of feedback from innovation partnerships. In recent years, the NYPD has developed a pilot program by which real-time sentiment data mining is integrated with their CompStat information. Police commanders understand that as they lead their forces to lower the rate of crime and victimization in their communities, a vital factor that must enter into this outcome is fostering trust and satisfaction from the public, while simultaneously keeping them safe.

Properly blending the metrics of performance management created by top policing experts with high-level data analytics that both monitor and evaluate trends that could result in social harm if ignored, enables police decision-makers to vastly increase their forecasting abilities. It also improves response time and the efficacy of that response when dealing with public order issues and crime. The development of methods that measure impact of police intervention and interaction can work exceptionally well in building levels of systemic accountability.

Mark founded a company, People Assistant, that offers a robust strategic planning system to support organizations as they build, monitor, track and report plan status. Figure 4 is an example of an electronic dashboard from People Assistant. It's a good example of what to measure and effectively monitor your plan.

Figure 4. People Assistant dashboard

Your plan should list the changes, a timeline for achieving the changes, and milestones to reach along the way. These are the points where you also schedule your celebrations — as each milestone is reached. Your plan should have a clearly defined process for measuring performance objectively.

STEP 5: CELEBRATE SUCCESSES TO REINFORCE CHANGE

5.1 THE PSYCHOLOGY OF SUCCESS

Successful people are driven to succeed. It's "in their leadership or personality DNA as well as their physical DNA."[75] Call it a "fire in their belly," or passion or whatever you like. But those who succeed don't do so by luck or accident. They literally have an in-born psychological need to achieve their goals from which comes their plan to achieve. [76] Status is important to them. It doesn't matter what the profession or level — patrol officer, lieutenant, or chief. They know what they want and pursue it.

We associate celebrating success with the reinforcement that we, the collective team, are headed in the right path, accomplishing mutually agreed goals together (simultaneously building a team through adversity and triumph). Celebrating success breeds more success. We build on the good, congratulating one another in the spirit of teamwork while also continuing to encourage and support each other not only for what we have just accomplished but what we are striving to achieve next.

We define success in several ways, including the direct measures of police performance commonly used that include crime rates, number of arrests and fines issued, clearance rates, and calls for service response time. Historically, these markers are inextricably connected to the perceived performance of a police department, however the future of policing must expand their view to encompass an accounting of police actions that go right.

Celebrate the times that officers and civilians survived highly charged encounters because the officers were superior thinkers in critical incidents. Celebrate the use of data in the laser-like focus on the slice of the population causing the greatest amount of harm and how those suspects are removed from the population without harming the rest of the community or the shine/luster of a police department.

We implemented a series of checks and balances through group meetings. We divided the work through assigned areas of responsibility under specific divisions – imagine a directorate or bureau. The workgroups followed an established list of timelines detailing milestones that we hoped to achieve.

Inclusive, the timelines also worked as our own accountability systems and provided everyone with advanced notice on the upcoming progress reporting periods. We had a visual aid that helped us see and track our progress on a display monitor, for example, the People Assistant dashboard (refer back to Figure 4).

Mark's role in those situations was to guide the conversation, facilitate dialogue that would challenge assumptions, ensure accurate reporting, and praise the progress. In some cases, he would ask more questions about issues that needed more analysis or something that either he wanted more answers to or somebody in the room probably had the same questions.

It's not just enough to recognize success. For it to have the power to reinforce the actions and decisions it must be understood then celebrated. The meetings also provided the chief with a clear view of the progress, the obstacles and the executive team's collaboration toward implementing the strategic plan.

Celebrating success

Recognizing and celebrating success is a very powerful motivator for individuals and teams. Number one, it reinforces the meaning behind all that hard work. Number two, if the successful employee or staff member is recognized for their success, it shows appreciation for their achievements, and conveys the critical message they matter, their hard work is noticed, and they are appreciated. This, in turn, boosts their self-esteem and it motivates them to pursue the next goal.

Think about an inspiring story or event you've read, or heard about. Did you feel inspired or motivated? Of course you did. Have you had a tough day on patrol, yet still managed to pull out a win? How does it feel to reflect on that, or to tell your colleagues or spouse? You don't have to save the world or have a huge win to feel motivated by a success. The small wins matter just the same. Sharing our successes helps us connect with each other and with the culture.

Recognizing the efforts and achievements of others with just a simple "Thank you," has been found to boost productivity by up to 50 percent.[77] You may not feel like it's appropriate to be a cheerleader 24/7, but as leaders it's up to us to create a culture where we show constant appreciation because everyone likes to be appreciated. It's one of the least expensive, yet most effective ways to impact your culture and influence employees. Whether you are calling or writing a note of appreciation, be specific, we've all been recipients of overly broad congratulatory notes and phone calls.

The fact that leaders take the time to point out a detail or two associated with the accomplishment (especially one directly tied to the values or the mission) are important. You are explicitly conveying that you took the time to read and understand the material, that's meaningful feedback.

Expressing gratitude has been shown to have significant positive effects on employees and their work/life balance. Showing gratitude and appreciation can increase a person's wellness, increase better sleep habits, increase metabolism and lessen stress.[78] Who needs that more than law enforcement? Celebrating success, expressing gratitude, and acknowledging effort directly impacts work results and employee interaction.[79]

The way that we celebrated success was either one success at a time or by clustering a number of successes. We would see events unfolding and the milestones that we were reaching and celebrate those successes.

As we began to put programs in place we also worked on a way to evaluate their effectiveness. We wanted to make sure that the programs we started were on the right track, stayed on track and reached the finish line.

That doesn't mean you can't acknowledge a success in roll call, or stop someone in the hall with a handshake, and "good job on _____." But celebrating your department's and your employee's successes is important in building a motivated culture. It's the job of every leader.

5.2 WHY CELEBRATION IS IMPORTANT: THE GOAL OF CELEBRATIONS

A pizza and cold soft drinks go a long way to boosting morale and celebrating successes. It's not the dollar value of recognition that matters. It's the sincerity and acknowledgment of a person or teams' efforts. When we finished the Patrol Officer 2025 Competency project, we bought pizza and soft drinks for every station on lunch and dinner breaks. We actually bought pizza and sodas for all four stations at 11:00 in the morning and then went back and did the same at 7:00 in the evening. That's an example of celebrating the success. We celebrated with the officers for completing the patrol officer competencies. It also gave us the opportunity to allow questions, listen to feedback and answer questions.

Celebrating goes back to the very basics of psychology. When you have a stimulus, there is a response. The stimulus, in this case, was the need for a different approach. The different approach we took was the patrol officer competencies to be successful. We developed the competencies that were adopted by the organization and the patrol officers. To reinforce that behavior we wanted to see occurring, right at the point where we introduced them, the officers accepted and were enrolled in the competency model, time after time Mark received positive feedback from the officers regarding their ability to provide input that would be a part of the strategic plan. If you've been around policing for any amount of time, you know that kind of feedback does not come easy.

We worked to teach and reinforce the competencies so that the improved behaviors of the officers continued. We changed the stimulus-response reinforcement we were doing. Eventually we moved from constant stimulus-response reinforcement to more intermittent reinforcement. We didn't have the funds to reinforce behavior every time it happened, so we turned to intermittent reinforcement — which can be more effective than constant reinforcement.

A lot of organizations can help celebrate behavior improvements with bonuses and pay, but we weren't able to do that. So we worked with what we had such as giving out T-shirts and button-down collared shirts with the name of our strategic plan or initiative embroidered into the shirt.

Never underestimate the power of appreciation, celebration, recognition or gratitude. It's not about the shirt, the pizza, the caps, or whatever. It's about the sincere, deeply appreciative words, deeds, actions and acknowledgement of a person's efforts, wins, and success. The more mature your organization, the more powerful the celebration.

The People Maturity Model

How mature is your organization? We've mentioned this before, but it's important to revisit it. When it comes to a "People Maturity Model," does your agency operate with intention and predictability — or is it immature, chaotic, and reactive?

Mature organizations, such as businesses and organizations may or may not have been around for decades. But they have been around long enough to understand how to put a strategic plan in place. They have developed competencies, created procedures that are replicable, obtained data that's displayed and operated the organization based on metrics. Police departments implement many of these strategies and tactics, but they don't aggregate and apply them against a performance model. We applied all of our strategies and tactics of Mark's suggested plan and then tied them back to this research-based model of greater performance.

Joel Trammell, CEO of Khorus Software, writing for INC Magazine, says "most companies exist somewhere between Levels 1 and 3. Companies at Level 4 are doing very well for themselves. But when you achieve Level 5, the organization operates at a whole different level: the leadership vision is clear, the mission engages and drives employees, and performance is consistent and predictable.[80] The definition below is easier to understand as it relates to an agency.

- Level 1: Confused. Any company vision exists only inside the Chief's head. He or she has not clearly communicated it to anyone else.

- Level 2: Described. The Chief shares a vision with a chosen few but cannot tell a story that resonates with anyone.

- Level 3: Declared. The majority of people understand the vision, but they aren't able to internalize it and let it guide their daily responsibilities.

- Level 4. Influenced. Everyone knows the story and understands how his or her functions contribute to implementation of the company's strategy.

- Level 5: Predictable. All employees own and act on the story and are emotionally connected to achieving the vision.

With the right coaching, instruction, and information you can mature your organization quickly.

5.3 THE RING DOORBELL PARTNERSHIP

Ring is a home security company with a device that lets you see, hear, and speak to people outside your front door from your phone, tablet, or Echo device. The company is owned by Amazon and it also works with Alexa. Home-owners have used it to prevent everything from package theft to home invasions from hundreds of miles away. Communities embraced the idea and by sharing their videos with the police department they could even help solve crimes.

Ramon learned about the Ring program early on and brought it back to the Mesa Police Department, which promoted it on its website:

> The Mesa Police Department is always looking for new and innovative ways to provide the best pos-sible service to our residents! We discovered that many people have installed doorbell cameras as an added layer of protection for their homes. As a result, we've partnered with Ring.com, which allows us to post and comment directly to the Neighbors app, send out real-time crime and

safety alerts, and even ask if residents have video they would like to share with us to help solve a crime! It's an additional Neighborhood Watch for our Mesa residents! Check it out today!

By becoming early adopters in the Ring technology and working with the Neighbors app, the department enjoyed great success that was celebrated across the community. Of course, it didn't go off without a hitch. There was national news to the effect that Ring was partnering with law enforcement agencies to create a surveillance state. Of course, police departments and Ring had to clarify their position that it wasn't the creation of a surveillance state. We had to jump this hurdle, but overall the program was well received.

It was exciting to be an early adopter in leveraging technology in this way. As a result of our success and the success of other early adopters you'll find many police departments and municipalities have adopted it.

When you create a community on the inside and then extend it out and embrace and pull in the outside, now you're talking about a collaborative co-creation or building of something that's mutually beneficial. You can build a successful supportive culture and then, eventually, you get into a maintenance mode and can keep revitalizing it again and again.

Ramon wanted officers to feel that they could accomplish their goals — that, together, they could accomplish anything. He wanted them to know that their work made a difference and to realize that they mattered to him and to the department's success.

5.5 BEYOND THE CELEBRATION: MOVING FORWARD THROUGH MASTERY AND MENTORING

A strategic plan and a list of goals and initiatives isn't something you put in place and check on once a year. Monitoring and training are ongoing. A successful strategic plan is about preparing for the future and finding ongoing solutions to current problems, and issues we haven't even imagined yet.

If you have a choice and a police department or any company where you have the capacity to bring in someone to help with a change or culture initiative, you would be much more successful if you hire a strategic consultant who is focused on the 20 percent— that strategic leverage point — that yields an 80 percent return.

It's about a vision for the future as both technology and human beings change and create a different society. It's a plan for growth, competency, community and confidence in police, and bonding and trust among citizens, leaders, the police and yes — politicians. We celebrate, but we don't sit back on our laurels and success and say, "Okay, that was fun."

We move forward — into mastery of the strategic plan, then into mentoring others so they too can create their own plans, and experience their own success.

Here are some of that challenges that police departments around the country are facing:

- Lack of shared vision (vision, mission, and values are not a part of daily work)
- Lack of confidence in leadership
- Lack of community support
- Lack of accountability
- Lack of trust
- Communication and coordination around twenty-first century challenges, such as video incidents
- Resources, especially patrol officers
- Long-range planning to address growth
- Training clearly aligned to mission
- Strategy model (refer back to Figure 2)

Any one of those items could keep you busy for months. How do we ensure that all of those issues are met, and met successfully? A well-designed and implemented strategic plan, a strategic council and a dashboard of plan status.

Implementing Your Strategy: Strategic Definitions

Your existing strategic plan should reach down and through your entire organization. It affects and relies on contributions from every employee and/or stakeholder. As long as it's taken you to create your plan, and as important as it is, for some reason, it may still not appear to be working. Why?

The reason there's a lack of an effective strategy, or the failure to execute an existing strategy in many police departments is simple:

- Little to no understanding of the importance of strategy
- An inability to effectively and clearly define a strategy
- Difficulty getting support for the strategy
- Lack of knowledge about how to implement the strategy
- Lack of an oversight or strategic council
- Lack of an adequate strategic plan tracking and reporting system

Having an articulated strategic plan, as well as understanding *how* to implement that plan is critical for any business, person, or agency.

At its core, implementation is simply understanding how to link people, strategy, and operations, the three core processes of every business or agency, together in a way that generates the desired results or goals.

In their book *Execution: The Discipline of Getting Things Done*, former CEO of General Electric Larry Bossidy and senior executive advisor Ram Charan said the key to proper execution lies in three core areas: **people, strategy and operations:**

"The people process is more important than either the strategy or operations processes," they wrote. "After all, it's the people of an organization who make judgments about how markets are changing, create strategies based on those judgments, and translate the strategies into operational realities."[81]

They wrote about business, but the fact is, it is people — especially in police work — that make the decisions that make the differences. Whether those decisions are made on the street, in the boardroom, or at top executive levels within any organization, effective implementation of an organization's strategies can make or break the organization.

Implementation done right is a disciplined process. It's a logical *set of connected activities by an organization to make their strategy work.* In *Making Strategy Work: Leading Effective Execution and Change,* Lawrence G. Hrebiniak wrote, "Without a careful, planned approach to execution, strategic goals cannot be attained." We agree.

SUMMARY

IN SUMMARY, WE BELIEVE that at this moment in time, the law enforcement profession has many challenges and great opportunities, policing professionals stand at the cusp of the reform era of policing and they must meet the moment with energy, creativity and resolve. John F. Kennedy said, "Life is never easy. There is work to be done and obligations to be met—obligations to truth, to justice, and to liberty." We firmly believe that any organization can meet the moment by understanding the values that define them and the communities they serve, to in turn create systems that enhance and support the pro-social goals of genuine public safety.

We say that values matter. If there's only one thing you take away from this book, that should be it. Values are the foundation your career, your family, your life, your department, and your contribution to your community are built upon. Without knowing them, living by them, and embracing them in everything you do, your path will be more challenging than you can imagine.

BEFORE YOU GO

Thank you so much for the opportunity to spend time with you, while you took time to read this book. We hope this book has inspired, motivated, taught you something new, and sparked ideas in you, the reader. We also hope you will create and launch your own strategic plan for your organization.

If you enjoyed this book and gained even just a few insights that were helpful to you, please share them with others. But most of all, please share what you felt were relevant and interesting on Amazon with a paragraph or two review. Amazon is where more than two-thirds of all books are sold. We would sincerely welcome your thoughts.

How to Leave a Review

Just go to Amazon (www.amazon.com), look up the title, and then type in a short review. Even if you only have read a couple of chapters, leaving reviews makes all the difference to the success of a book. Your impressions and takeaways matter.

In our content-cluttered world, books succeed by the kind, generous time readers take to leave honest reviews. Thank you in advance for this kind gesture. And, finally, if you would like to reach out to us with questions or comments about the book or to schedule a consultation or meeting, contact us via our website, www.donoharm-book.org.

IN MEMORIAM

"In memoriam" is a Latin phrase equivalent to "in memory (of)," referring to remembering or honoring a deceased person. While we don't condone the unwise lifestyle choices and decisions some people on either side of the law make, we do remember they were/are someone's son, daughter, mother, sister, or someone's father, someone's friend, and someone's brother. They were important to— and loved by— someone.

We have a justice system where our peers, and our courts, and our community review the facts of a case and decide if a person is guilty or not. It is not up to police officers to make that judgement. However, officers may sometimes be called up to defend their lives, or the lives of others, or to make choices and take actions others don't understand that result in the death or injury of another. There are no simple or "one explanation fits all" answers. That's what makes life complex, challenging, and often bittersweet. It's also why we have a justice system, as imperfect as it can seem sometimes—it is the best in the world.

We have chosen to remember both citizens and officers here. We remember them for being human beings—imperfect, troubled, and perhaps struggling, but having the potential to change direction and their lives right up until the time they died. Remembering someone is not about defending their actions or choices, or about judging them. It's about taking time to acknowledge the humanity in them, in all of us—and the potential each of us has to make or reject good decisions.

The fact is we value life because it is a life—not a white life, a black life, a blue life—but a life. And life, no matter who you are, is fragile. That is why we remember those who died in police custody or from police aggression as well as we remember the officers ambushed, murdered, or killed from the riots and protests that followed. Life matters.

To the officers we've known or met or worked with, we thank you. If you are a police officer or related to, or know a police officer, thank you for your service, your heart, your dedication. It's a challenging time to be in law enforcement, and we know that. We've written this book in hopes of helping improve the system, the training, and the outcomes of future encounters between civilians, communities and the police. It's been a deadly decade. Things need to change, and we believe they are—sadly enough, after too many deaths, too much violence, and too many poor or inappropriate decisions. Both civilian and law enforcement have erred in their choices and actions, and blame doesn't change the past.

We want to take the time and space to acknowledge, honor, and thank all those law enforcement officers, security, fire and rescue and EMTs killed, died, or injured during the last decade. Those who protect our communities, cities, and the culture and lives often pay a dear price for what they do.

We also want to acknowledge the civilians and citizens who have died during encounters with police officers—rightly or wrongly. We're not here to take sides, assign blame, or play judge or jury. We want to acknowledge that LIFE is precious and that the loss of any life, no matter the circumstances, is tragic. No one deserves to die or be harmed in the process of laws being enforced. That doesn't mean bad things don't happen. They do.

But that doesn't mean we can't draw value, lessons, and change from them. If we don't, their lives have been lost, damaged, or changed in vain.

What leaders do when mistakes are made:

- **Leaders acknowledge their mistakes.** Don't hide, justify, or quantify what happened. Admit your mistake, take responsibility. Vulnerability is the ultimate strength.

- **Leaders learn from their mistakes.** As the old saying goes, when you repeat a mistake it is not a mistake anymore but a decision. Mistakes are the way we learn. Sometimes the consequences are minor, sometimes they're life altering. Either way, leaders learn from them and apply them to the next situation.

- **Leaders teach others from what they've learned from their mistakes.** We'd all rather learn from the mistakes of others rather than from personal experience. It's less painful! So don't let your lesson go to waste. Teach others. That's what being a police training officer is all about—teaching others from your experience and mistakes.

- **Move beyond your mistake.** It does no one any good to wallow in their mistakes. Keep moving forward, keep learning, keep changing, keep improving.[82]

Honor all who have given their energy, time, and lives in any way to protect their community. Remember and respect those who have given their all, those who have lost their lives, and those who have suffered from all sides and all communities. We have. We will. We will continue to do so.

ACKNOWLEDGMENTS

Ramon Batista

There are so many people who have helped me get to where I am today that I can't name them all. However, there are a few individuals who made specific and long-lasting changes that impacted me in ways too great not to call out. First and foremost, there's my amazing wife, Aninna. She's always by my side and able to shed light on the issues that I missed while being the rock of the family. No one knows better than a chief's wife what the demands are on time and energy to be at our best; a chief's wife lives through the highs and lows of the profession. I couldn't do it without her love and support. Thank you, Aninna.

My first Sergeant, Phil Corrigan, taught me to think about the great power and influence I had as a police officer. He taught me that in an instant, I could impact someone's life forever. It was not until so many years later that I realized just how far ahead he was in his thinking and his teachings as a police supervisor—keeping young cops from making really dumb mistakes.

Chief Brett Klein, a consummate professional, told me the hard truths about policing, and supported me while exposing me to greater responsibilities. In a crisis, there was none better. He taught me to stay focused and tell the truth.

Then, there is the Police Executive Research Forum and the Major Cities Chiefs Association. Through my affiliation with you, my views around policing, values, responsibility and community were expanded. Your dedicated work continues, there are many more like me that need your guidance as we collectively work toward improving our profession.

I'd like to acknowledge all the dedicated men and women in policing who put their uniform on and kiss their families goodbye every day, with the promise that they'll be courageous and safe. They go out with the best intentions to deal with a plethora of social issues they did not create in a justice system they did not build. To all the good officers, that care, show empathy and bravery in their darkest hour, you are my heroes.

Mark Ziska

This book would not be possible without the challenges and opportunities throughout my career. I'm very grateful to all the following people:

First and foremost, thank you to my wife, Marcy Ziska, my inspiration. She challenged me to look deeply within to understand that even without my conscious knowledge I carried inherent bias. That we all do. Some bias was on the surface and some more embedded. Without her help and positive challenges, I would never have understood this difficult concept of bias and to be able to translate those learnings to this book. She carries my heart in her heart.

Joe Pennisi, president of Hughes Naval and Maritime Systems, a great leader and mentor who flipped a switch in me to make the change from being a tactician to a strategist. I'm forever grateful to him for creating possibilities.

Mark Carneal, Innovative Resources, who was there when I needed him and led me in my transition to embracing strategy and leadership. He taught me the strategy model.

Perry Shazier, a friend and colleague who took me through "the talk" that he and other African American parents must have with their children. He has also become a sounding board for me on racial sensitivity and understanding.

Traci Tolliver, the ultimate researcher. Traci amazed us with her research abilities finding peer-review and research-based material to reinforce our intuitive beliefs.

Becky Blanton for daily generating new ideas, stories and making writing a book a fun adventure. You are an amazing person. You taught us that "hope finds a way!" Easy to say but more difficult to understand. We recommend others to join the millions who have watched her TEDGlobal Talk.

And finally, Melissa G. Wilson, our book-creation expert, coach, and project manager, who led a team of experts to complete our first book as well as guide a couple of reluctant writers step by step through the arduous process of book writing. Thank you also for your confidence in us and your steadfast leadership in getting our idea and thoughts into this book that we're so proud of.

ENDNOTES

1   Olivia B. Waxman, "How the US Got Its Police Force," Time, May 18, 2017, https://time.com/4779112/police-history-origins/.

2   Waxman, "Police Force."

3   Hubert Williams and Patrick V. Murphy, "The Evolving Strategy of Police: A Minority View," NCJS.gov. Accessed September 24, 2020. https://www.ncjrs.gov/pdffiles1/nij/121019.pdf.

4   Oklahoma Historical Society. "Tulsa Race Massacre." https://www.okhistory.org/publications/enc/entry.php?entry=TU013

5   Jacqui Shine, "'Dragnet' Was Straight-Up LAPD Propaganda, on National TV for Years," Timeline, June 20, 2017. https://timeline.com/dragnet-lapd-propaganda-cop-bb19d9a5fb6f.

6   James Queally, "Watts Riots: Traffic Stop Was the Spark That Ignited Days of Destruction in LA," LA Times, July 29, 2015, https://www.latimes.com/local/lanow/la-me-ln-watts-riots-explainer-20150715-htmlstory.

html#:~:text=The%20chaos%20that%20enveloped%20South,damaged%20by%20fires%20or%20looting.

7   "Watts Rebellion," History, June 24, 2020, https://www.history.com/topics/1960s/watts-riots.

8   Barnhill, "Watts Riot."

9   Queally, "Watts Riots."

10 "The President's Task Force on 21st Century Policing," accessed September 24, 2020, https://cops.usdoj.gov/pdf/taskforce/taskforce_finalreport.pdf.

11 President's Task Force.

12 Tom R. Tyler, "Why People Obey the Law." Princeton University Press. Accessed September 24, 2020.https://press.princeton.edu/books/paperback/9780691126739/why-people-obey-the-law

13 "Section 1983 Lawsuit - How to Bring a Civil Rights Claim," Shouse California Law Group, updated August 10, 2020. https://www.shouselaw.com/ca/civil-rights/1983-lawsuits/#:~:

14 "Civil Rights in the United States," University of Minnesota Law School, accessed September 27, 2020. https://libguides.law.umn.edu/c.php?g=125765&p=2893387#:~:text=Section%201983%20provides%20an%20individual,civil%20rights%20that%20already%20exist.

15 "People with Untreated Mental Illness 16 Times More Likely to Be Killed by Law Enforcement," Treatment Advocacy Center, accessed September 6, 2020,

https://www.treatmentadvocacycenter.org/key-issues/criminalization-of-mental-illness/2976-people-with-untreated-mental-illness-16-times-more-likely-to-be-killed-by-law-enforcement-

16 "LAPD Use of Force Year-End Review Executive Summary 2015," Los Angeles Police Department, accessed September 6, 2020, http://lapd-assets.lapdonline.org/assets/pdf/UOF%20Executive%20Summary.pdf.

17 "Mass Shootings in the United States between 1982 and February 2020, by presence of prior signs of shooter's mental health issues." Statista.com. July 31, 2020. https://www.statista.com/statistics/811557/us-mass-shootings-by-prior-signs-of-shooter-s-mental-health-issues

18 Azza AbuDagga, Sidney Wolfe, Michael Carome, Amanda Phatdouang, and E. Fuller Torrey, "Individuals with Serious Mental Illnesses in County Jails: A Survey of Jail Staff's Perspectives," Public Citizen and Treatment Advocacy Center, July 14, 2016, https://www.treatmentadvocacycenter.org/storage/documents/jail-survey-report-2016.pdf.

19 Thomas Breen, "95.6% of Cops' Calls Don't Involve Violence," New Haven Independent, June 19, 2020,

https://www.newhavenindependent.org/index.php/
archives/entry/police_dispatch_stats.

20   Bureau of Justice Statistics. "Contacts Between
the Police and the Public, 2015." BJS.gov. Accessed
September 6, 2020. 0 https://www.bjs.gov/index.
cfm?ty=pbdetail&iid=6406#:~:text=The%20
portion%20of%20U.S.%20residents,62.9%20
million%20to%2053.5%20million).

21   Bureau of Justice Statistics. "Contacts Between the
Police and the Public, 2015." BJS.gov. Accessed September 6, 2020. https://www.bjs.gov/content/pub/pdf/
cpp15.pdf

22   President's Task Force on 21st Century Policing. "Final
Report of the President's Task Force on 21st Century
Policing." Cops.usdoj-gov. https://cops.usdoj.gov/pdf/
taskforce/taskforce_finalreport.pdf

23   Gary Riccio, Randall Sullivan, Gerald Klein, Mar-
garet Salter, and Henry Kinnison, "Warrior Ethos:
Analysis of the Concept and Initial Development of
Applications," US Army Research Institute for the
Behavioral and Social Sciences, accessed September
6, 2020, https://www.hsdl.org/?view&did=21479.

24   Military Leadership Diversity Commission. "Department of Defense Core Values." Diveristy.defense.gov.
Accessed September 6, 2020. https://diversity.defense.
gov/Portals/51/Documents/Resources/Commission/

docs/Issue% 20Papers/Paper%2006%20-%20DOD%20 Core%20Values.pdf.

25   Military Leadership Diversity Commission.

26   Val van Brocklin, "Warriors vs. Guardians: A Seismic Shift in Policing or Just Semantics?" Police1, May 7, 2019, "https://www.police1.com/21st-century-policing-task-force/articles/warriors-vs-guardians-a-seismic-shift-in-policing-or-just-semantics-EXB-kY2pEWCHi6Mni

27   Van Brocklin.

28   Power DMS Blog. "Adopting the Guardian Mindset." Powerdms.com. July 14, 2017. https://www.powerdms.com/blog/adopting-the-guardian-mindset

29   Patrick Oliver, "Hiring in the Spirit of Service," Cedarville University History and Government Faculty Publications, 2002, https://digitalcommons.cedarville.edu/cgi/viewcontent.cgi?article=1122&context=history_and_government_publications.

30   Oliver.

31   Candice Norwood, "Calls for Reform Bring Renewed Focus to Community Policing, But Does It Work?" PBS, September 18, 2020, https://www.pbs.org/newshour/politics/calls-for-reform-bring-renewed-focus-to-community-policing-but-does-it-work.

32   Seth Stoughton, "Law Enforcement's "Warrior" Problem," Harvard Law Review, April 10, 2015, https://

harvardlawreview.org/2015/04/law-enforcements-warrior-problem.

33   Lydia Saad, "Black Americans Want Police to Retain Local Presence," Gallup, August 5, 2020, https://news.gallup.com/poll/316571/black-americans-police-retain-local-presence.aspx?utm_source=tagrss&utm_medium=rss&utm_campaign=syndication.

34   Marcel Schwantes, "Research Has Revealed the 5 Top Behaviors That Fortune 500 Companies Like Apple, Amazon, and Microsoft Live By," Inc. August 8, 2019, https://www.inc.com/marcel-schwantes/research-has-revealed-5-top-behaviors-that-fortune-500-companies-like-apple-amazon-microsoft-live-by.html.

35   Eric Christopher, "How Establishing Core Values Drives Success," Entrepreneur, March 20, 2017. https://www.entrepreneur.com/article/290078.

36   Ben Parr, "Amazon Acquires Zappos for $850 Million," Mashable, July 22, 2009, https://mashable.com/2009/07/22/amazon-buys-zappos.

37   Robert Chestnut, "How to Build a Company that Actually Values Integrity," Harvard Business Review, July 30, 2020, https://hbr.org/2020/07/how-to-build-a-company-that-actually-values-integrity

38   Chestnut.

39   Chestnut.

40 Steve Denning, "Why Leadership Storytelling Is Important," Forbes, June 8, 2011, https://www.forbes.com/sites/stevedenning/2011/06/08/why-leadership-storytelling-is-important/#45072ffe780f.

41 Michael Macaulay and Mike Rowe, "Happy Ever After? Making Sense of Narrative in Creating Police Values," Public Management Review 22 (9), 1306–23, https://doi.org/10.1080/14719037.2019.1630474.

42 Chris Sibley, "New Zealand Attitudes and Values Study," University of Auckland, accessed September 27, 2020, https://www.psych.auckland.ac.nz/en/about/new-zealand-attitudes-and-values-study.html

43 Sibley.

44 Macaulay and Rowe.

45 Anna North, "Do Americans Support Defunding Police?" Vox, June 23, 2020, https://www.vox.com/2020/6/23/21299118/defunding-the-police-minneapolis-budget-george-floyd.

46 James Gallagher, "'Memories' Pass between Generations," BBC News, December 1, 2013, https://www.bbc.com/news/health-25156510#:~:text.

47 Gallagher.

48 James Q. Wilson, "The DNA of Politics," City Journal, winter 2009, https://www.city-journal.org/html/dna-politics-13148.html.

49 Police Executive Research Forum, "Re-engineering Training on Police Use of Force." Police Forum, accessed September 6, 2020, https://www.policeforum.org/assets/reengineeringtraining1.pdf.

50 "Procedural Justice and Building the Guardian Mindset Starts Internally as the Ultimate Liability Protector," Daigle Law Group, October 6, 2018, https://daiglelawgroup.com/procedural-justice-and-building-the-guardian-mindset-starts-internally-as-the-ultimate-liability-protector.

51 George Wood, Tom R. Tyler, and Andrew V. Papachristos, "Procedural Justice Training Reduces Police Use of Force and Complaints Against Officers," PNAS 117 (18), 9815–21, www.pnas.org/cgi/doi/10.1073/pnas.1920671117.

52 Rachel Smith, "Strategy vs. Tactics: The Main Difference and How to Track Progress of Both," ClearPoint Strategy. Accessed September 6, 2020. https://www.clearpointstrategy.com/strategy-vs-tactics.

53 Robert Wasserman and Mark H. Moore, "Values In Policing," US Department of Justice, accessed September 6, 2020. https://www.publicsafety.gc.ca/lbrr/archives/cnmcs-plcng/cn32582-eng.pdf.

54 Rashad Robinson, "Normalizing Injustice," Color of Change Hollywood, January 2020, https://hollywood.

colorofchange.org/wp-content/uploads/2020/02/Normalizing-Injustice_Complete-Report-2.pdf.

55 Stephen M.R. Covey with Rebecca R. Merrill, The Speed of Trust (New York: Free Press, 2018).

56 Insightlink, "Why Trust Matters in the Workplace," Insightlink, accessed September 6, 2020, https://www.insightlink.com/why-trust-matters-in-the-workplace.html#.

57 Insightlink.

58 Crowe Associates, "The Importance of Trust in Teams." Crowe Associates, accessed September 6, 2020, http://www.crowe-associates.co.uk/teams-and-groups/the-importance-of-trust-in-teams.

59 Daniel Pink, Drive: The Surprising Truth about What Motivates Us (New York: Riverhead Books, 2009).

60 Pink.

61 Pink.

62 Community Oriented Policing Services, "Building Trust," US Department of Justice, accessed September 6, 2020, https://cops.usdoj.gov/buildingtrust.

63 "Law Enforcement Code of Ethics," International Association of Chiefs of Police, accessed September 6, 2020. https://www.theiacp.org/resources/law-enforcement-code-of-ethics.

64   Paul J. Zak, "How Our Brains Decide When to Trust," Harvard Business Review, July 18, 2019, https://hbr.org/2019/07/how-our-brains-decide-when-to-trust.

65   Stephen Dimmock and William C. Gerken, "Research: How One Bad Employee Can Corrupt a Whole Team," Harvard Business Review, March 5, 2018, https://hbr.org/2018/03/research-how-one-bad-employee-can-corrupt-a-whole-team.

66   Used with permission from Patricia MacCorquodale, Professor and Dean Emerita of the Honors College, University of Arizona.

67   Sigal Barsade, "Five Steps for Managing Culture Change," University of Pennsylvania Wharton Executive Education. Accessed September 6, 2020. https://executiveeducation.wharton.upenn.edu/thought-leadership/wharton-at-work/2014/09/managing-culture-change/#:~.

68   Barsade.

69   Barak Ariel, Alex Sutherland, Darren Henstock, Josh Young, and Gabriela Sosinski, "The Deterrence Spectrum: Explaining Why Police Body-Worn Cameras 'Work' or 'Backfire' in Aggressive Police–Public Encounters," Semantic Scholar, accessed October 1, 2020, https://pdfs.semanticscholar.org/70f5/fd94d7aa49702030ba5010332191a2018714.pdf?_ga=2.83335446.1659982729.1601532873-1022416011.1601532873.

70 Alex Sutherland, Barak Ariel, William Farrar, and Randy De Anda, "Post-Experimental Follow-ups— Fade-out Versus Persistence Effects: The Rialto Police Body-Worn Camera Experiment Four Years On." Journal of Criminal Justice 53 (2017), 110–16, https://doi.org/10.1016/j.jcrimjus.2017.09.008.

71 Mindtools Blog. "Action Plans, Small Scale Planning." Mindtools.com. Accessed September 7, 2020. https://www.mindtools.com/pages/article/newHTE_04.htm

72 Steven L. Bernstein, June Weiss, and Leslie Curry, "Visualizing Implementation: Contextual and Organizational Support Mapping of Stakeholders (COSMOS)," Implementation Science Communications, May 27, 2020. https://implementationsciencecomms.biomedcentral.com/articles/10.1186/s43058-020-00030-8

73 NCJRS.gov. "Understanding Community Policing: A Framework for Action." Bureau of Justice Assistance. Accessed October 1, 2020. https://www.ncjrs.gov/pdffiles/commp.pdf

74 Cameron S. McLay, "Building Police Legitimacy through Measuring and Managing Performance," National Police Foundation, accessed September 22, 2020, https://www.policefoundation.org/building-police-legitimacy-through-measuring-and-managing-performance/.

75 Gallagher.

76   Gallagher.

77   Adler Display, "Employee Appreciation Programs
      That Work: Why a Recognition Wall Should be Part
      of Your Plan." Adler Display, May 14, 2019, https://
      www.adlerdisplay.com/employee-appreciation-pro-
      grams-that-work-why-a-recognition-wall-should-
      be-part-of-your-plan

78   O.C. Tanner, "The Psychological Effects of Workplace
      Appreciation and Gratitude." Emergenetics, accessed
      September 6, 2020, https://www.emergenetics.com/
      blog/workplace-appreciation-gratitude.

79   Tanner.

80   Joe Trammell, "How Mature Is Your Organization?
      Use This Model to Find Out," Inc., November 7, 2016,
      https://www.inc.com/joel-trammell/how-to-gauge-
      your-organizations-maturity-using-your-ceo-as-the-
      benchmark.html.

81   Larry Bossidy and Ram Charan, Execution: The Dis-
      cipline of Getting Things Done (New York: Crown
      Business, 2002).

82   Lolly Daskal, "4 Impressive Ways Great Leaders
      Handle Their Mistakes," Inc., April 23, 2018, https://
      www.inc.com/lolly-daskal/4-impressive-ways-great-
      leaders-handle-their-mistakes.html.

Made in the USA
Monee, IL
23 February 2021

61146442R10136